The
WORST-CASE SCENARIO
Survival Handbook:
EXTREME EDITION

By Joshua Piven and David Borgenicht
Illustrations by Brenda Brown

CHRONICLE BOOKS

SAN FRANCISCO

Library of Congress Cataloging-in-Publication Data available.

ISBN: 0-8118-4538-9

Manufactured in Canada

Designed by Frances J. Soo Ping Chow
Illustrations by Brenda Brown

Typeset in Adobe Caslon, Bundesbahn Pi, and Zapf Dingbats

A **QUIRK** Book
Visit www.worstcasescenarios.com

Distributed in Canada by Raincoast Books
9050 Shaughnessy Street
Vancouver, British Columbia V6P 6E5

10 9 8 7 6 5 4 3 2 1

Chronicle Books LLC
85 Second Street
San Francisco, California 94105
www.chroniclebooks.com

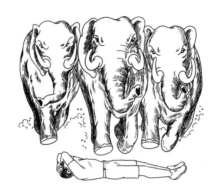

The
WORST-CASE SCENARIO
Survival Handbook:
EXTREME EDITION

WARNING

When a life is imperiled or a dire situation is at hand, safe alternatives may not exist. To deal with the extreme worst-case scenarios presented in this book, we highly recommend—insist, actually—that the best course of action is to consult a professionally trained expert. But because highly trained professionals may not always be available when the safety or sanity of individuals is at risk, we have asked experts on various subjects to describe the techniques they might employ in these emergency situations. THE PUBLISHER, AUTHORS, AND EXPERTS DISCLAIM ANY LIABILITY from any injury that may result from the use, proper or improper, of the information contained in this book. All the information in this book comes from experts in the situation at hand, but we do not guarantee that the information contained herein is complete, safe, or accurate, nor should it be considered a substitute for your good judgment and common sense. And finally, nothing in this book should be construed or interpreted to infringe on the rights of other persons or to violate criminal statutes; we urge you to obey all laws and respect all rights, including property rights, of others.

—The Authors

CONTENTS

The calamity that comes is never the one
we had prepared ourselves for.

—Mark Twain

As soon as there is life there is danger.

—Ralph Waldo Emerson

The minute you think you've got it made,
disaster is just around the corner.

—Joe Paterno

INTRODUCTION

We are dismayed and sorry to report that despite our best efforts, the world hasn't really gotten any safer.

We tried, with the publication of the first *Worst-Case Scenario Survival Handbook* in 1999, to give readers the expertise and the confidence to survive life's sudden turns for the worse. Our approach was simple:

1. Be prepared.
2. Don't panic.
3. Have a plan.

That first book provided plans for dealing with quicksand, killer bees, leaps from rooftops, and many other misadventures.

We followed up with *The Worst-Case Scenario Survival Handbook: Travel,* which proved enormously helpful for anyone leaving their house, and then diversified, providing survival techniques for entirely different kinds of dangers: *Dating & Sex, Golf, Holidays, Work, Parenting, College,* and *Weddings.*

With this handbook we return to our roots— good old-fashioned, action-packed survival for those inclined to extreme activities that go bad.

Within, you'll find all-new advice about surviving dozens of scenarios, from an elephant stampede to a runaway hot air balloon, from skiing off a 100-foot drop to landing a helicopter if the engine fails. You'll learn how to survive if you're stranded on an iceberg, if you fall down a street grating, and if you find your-self choking or having a heart attack. All the advice is backed by our network of experts, and all comes with clear, step-by-step, illustrated instructions.

Because, after all this time, after the TV show and the calendars and journals and cards and games, we still want you to be prepared. And, trust us, you're not as prepared as you could be.

Because you just never know. . . .

—The Authors

CHAPTER I
ANIMAL ATTACKS

HOW TO SURVIVE AN ELEPHANT STAMPEDE

⭐ Take available cover.
Elephants stampede when they are startled by a loud noise or to escape a perceived threat. If the elephants are running away from a threat but toward you, do not try to outrun them. Elephants can run at a speed in excess of 25 mph. Even while charging, they can make sharp turns and are able to climb steep slopes. Seek a sturdy structure close by and take cover.

⭐ Climb a tree.
The elephants are likely to avoid trees when running. Grab a branch at its base and use your legs to power yourself up the tree, keeping three of your limbs in contact with the tree at all times as you climb. If you cannot climb the tree, stand behind it. Elephants will avoid large obstacles when running.

⭐ Lie down.
Unless the elephant is intent on trampling you, because you are hunting or the elephant thinks you are hunting, elephants typically avoid stepping on a prone human being, even while charging.

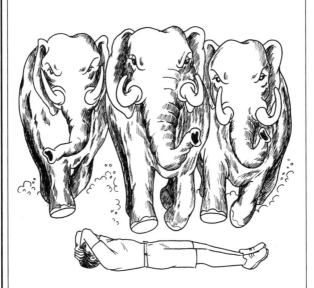

If you cannot find cover, lie down. Elephants typically avoid stepping on a prone human being, even while charging.

 Protect your face.

Do not get up immediately. After the threat has passed, an elephant may show great interest in the apparently dead bodies of humans and may attempt to "bury" you under tree branches, leaves, and dirt. If you sense an elephant moving above you, lie still and cover your face with your hands. The rough skin on the elephant's trunk may cause severe abrasions if it rubs against you.

Be Aware

- An angry elephant will tuck its ears back and curl its trunk up, away from danger.
- If the elephants are angry at you, they may attempt to spear you with their tusks and then fling your body.
- If the last human the elephant met was a hunter/poacher, it will be more likely to treat you as a threat and attempt an attack.

HOW TO
ESCAPE FROM A
CHARGING RHINO

★ Climb a tree.
See "How to Survive an Elephant Stampede," on page 16.

★ Run for scrub.
A rhino probably will not follow you into thick scrub brush. Get as far in as possible. Adrenaline will prevent you from noticing the painful thorns until you try to get out.

★ Stand your ground and shout.
If no tree or scrub is available to allow your escape, stand and face the animal (rhinos have poor eyesight but are attracted to movement). As the rhino approaches, scream and shout as loud as you can. A charging rhino may veer away from a noisy target.

★ Run in the opposite direction.
A rhino will continue running in the same direction when it is charging and is not likely to turn around and come back for another attack. Once you have evaded the charge and the rhino has veered off, run in the opposite direction.

A charging rhino may avoid a noisy target.

Be Aware

- A surprised or startled rhino's first instinct is to charge a threat, whether real or imagined.
- A mother rhino will aggressively defend a calf by charging any and all threats.
- Rhinos can climb steep slopes and will also charge into water or mud.
- A rhino will charge and attack a vehicle and may chase one for more than a mile. A large male (5,000 pounds or more) can easily knock over a car.
- African black rhinos are generally considered the most dangerous and likely to charge, though white and Indian rhinos will also charge. Javan and Sumatran rhinos are smaller, shier, forest-dwelling, and considered less dangerous to humans.
- A white rhino's anterior (front) horn can be as long as 62 inches.

HOW TO OUTWIT
A PACK OF WOLVES

1 Slowly move to solid terrain.

In winter, wolves tend to chase their prey into deep snow or onto frozen lakes, surfaces where the hooves of the victim sink or slide. The wolves' large, padded feet give them a tremendous range-of-movement advantage in these areas. If you see wolves around you, slowly walk toward solid ground. Do not crouch down, and do not run. Even during warmer months, wolves will readily chase prey over solid ground and are capable of bursts of high speed, as fast as 35 mph over short distances. You cannot outrun a wolf.

2 Observe the wolves' posture.

A wolf can attack from any position, but a tail straight up in the air and ears pricked up are a signal of dominance and often indicate that the wolf is preparing to attack.

3 Charge one member of the pack.

Wolves are generally timid around humans and have a strong flight response. Running toward one wolf while yelling may scare it and the other members of the pack away from you.

4 Throw sticks and rocks.

If the wolves continue with an attack, throw sticks and rocks at those closest to you. Wolves tend to attack the lower portions of their victims' bodies in an attempt to hobble and then bring them to the ground. Kick or hit the wolves as they approach your legs until you scare them off.

Be Aware

- Captive wolves are more likely to attack a human than wolves in the wild. Attacks are often a dominance display. Captive wolves may attack and then eat a person.
- Solitary wolves are generally considered more of an attack threat to humans than pack wolves, though a pack of wolves can inflict more damage more quickly.
- Wild wolves habituated to the presence of humans are more likely to attack, since they have lost their fear of people.
- Wolves may hunt at any hour of the day or night.
- The bite pressure of an adult wolf is about 1,500 pounds per square inch. By contrast, the bite pressure of a German shepherd is about 500 pounds per square inch.
- A wolf pack may have 30 members.

HOW TO ESCAPE FROM A GIANT OCTOPUS

1 Pull away quickly.

In many cases, a human can escape from the grasp of a small- to medium-sized octopus by just swimming away. Propel yourself forward to create a pulling pressure on the octopus's arms. If you cannot get away, or if you feel yourself being pulled back, continue to the next step.

2 Do not go limp.

Octopi are naturally curious and, if strong enough, will check to see if you are a food item before letting you go. Do not act passively, or you may be bitten or quickly enveloped by the octopus's web, a flexible sheath used to trap prey. Once you are caught in a "web-over," escape will be extremely difficult. However, octopi tire easily, so continue to put pressure on the arms by attempting to swim away. The octopus may decide to let you go rather than bring you in for a closer look.

3 Prevent the octopus's arms from wrapping around your arms.

Initially, the octopus will secure itself to a rock or coral formation and reach out to grab you with just one or two arms. Once it has a firm grip on you, it will move you toward its mouth (called a "beak") by transferring you to the next sucker up the arm. Do not allow the first two octopus arms to pin your own arms to your sides, or you will have little chance of fighting it off.

4 Peel the suckers from your body.
Using your hands, start at the tip of each octopus arm and remove each successive sucker from your body, like peeling up a bath mat. Once you have loosened one of the octopus's arms, give it a spear, raft, surfboard, or other object to latch on to. Work quickly, before the suckers reattach to your body or the octopus's other arms have a chance to grab you.

5 Detach the octopus from its anchor.
Using the sucker removal method described in step 4, separate the octopus from its anchor. Octopi prefer to be anchored to a fixed object, and may swim away once dislodged.

6 Turn somersaults in the water.
If you have detached the octopus from its mooring but are still being held, turn your body in circles in the water to irritate it into releasing you.

7 Swim toward the surface.
Octopi dislike air intensely and will release you once they break the surface. Continue to peel the octopus's suckers from your body as you swim.

Peel the suckers starting from the tip of the octopus's arm.

Be Aware

- A giant Pacific octopus may be well over 100 pounds, with an arm span of 23 feet.
- Giant octopi are extremely strong, but do not constrict prey to kill: They tear victims with their sharp beaks.
- Giant Pacific octopi are not poisonous, though bites may become infected.
- Octopi typically eat crabs and clams, though they may eat fish and birds, and may bite at anything.
- Without training or free-diving experience, a swimmer will typically be able to hold his or her breath for only about a minute before losing consciousness.

HOW TO ESCAPE FROM AN ANGRY GORILLA

1 Evaluate the gorilla's behavior.
A stressed or angry gorilla is likely to vocalize loudly and pound, jump, or slap the ground before attacking. A gorilla that is just tugging at clothes or grabbing at you may simply be curious.

2 Do not react.
Do not scream, hit, or otherwise antagonize the gorilla. Even if the gorilla grabs you, it may be playful behavior. Scaring or aggravating the gorilla may provoke an angry response.

3 Be submissive.
Do not look directly at the gorilla. Remain quiet. Do not shout or open arms wide to try to appear larger. The gorilla may interpret these acts as hostile.

4 Watch for a bluff charge.
A gorilla may make a "bluff charge" before an attack to scare potential threats. It may scream or "bark," stomp its hands on the ground, and tear at vegetation as it advances toward you. A bluff charge is fast and intimidating and resembles an actual attack.

Groom the gorilla's arm to relax its grip.

5 Crouch down and make yourself as small a target as possible.

If the gorilla feels threatened during a bluffing display, it may decide to follow through with an attack.

6 Stay quiet and submissive.

An attack may include severe biting and pounding or tearing with the gorilla's hands. Even if it appears that the gorilla means to harm you, do not actively resist or fight back: It will interpret this behavior as threatening and may attack more severely.

7 | Groom.
If the gorilla has gotten hold of you, begin to "groom" its arm while loudly smacking your lips. Primates are fastidious groomers, and grooming the gorilla in this fashion may distract the gorilla in a nonthreatening way. As the gorilla's grip relaxes, slowly move your grooming hand to the gorilla's hand, showing keen interest in any bits of leaf or dirt on the gorilla.

8 | Remain quiet and passive until the gorilla loses interest or until help arrives.

Be Aware
If the gorilla has you in its grip, do not attempt to pry the gorilla's fingers apart to remove his hand. A full-grown silverback gorilla is much stronger than any adult human. The gorilla's grip will be like a vise that is impossible to open.

HOW TO ESCAPE FROM FIRE ANTS

1 Brush the ants off.

Fire ants inject venom from a stinger connected to a poison gland. A single ant will pinch the skin with its jaws and sting numerous times, injecting more venom with each sting. As the venom enters the skin, you will experience the intense, burning sensation that gives fire ants their name. Using your hand or a cloth, make a fast, sharp, brushing motion until their jaws dislodge from the skin and they fall off. Jumping up and down, shaking the affected area, and placing the ants under running water will not prevent the ants from attacking and may cause further injury.

2 Run from the area.

As you remove the ants, flee the area of the attack. When a mound or nest is disturbed, or foraging fire ants are encountered, they immediately climb up any vertical surface and sting. Hundreds of ants may attack within seconds, especially in mild to high temperatures, when ants stay closer to the surface. The ants will continue to attack even after you have left the nest area, however. Continue brushing them as you run.

3 Remove your clothing.

Fire ants will stay in the creases of clothing and may sting later. Once you have reached safety and removed all visible ants, take off your shoes, socks, pants, and any other articles of clothing where the ants were visible. Inspect your clothes carefully, especially the pockets and seams, before putting them back on. If possible, launder the items before wearing them again.

4 | Treat the affected area.
After several minutes, the site of each bite will redden and swell into a bump. A topical antihistamine may relieve some itching at bite sites. Several hours to several days later, the bumps will become white, fluid-filled pustules, which will last for several days or, in some cases, weeks. Immediately upon the appearance of pustules, treat the affected areas with a solution of half bleach, half water to lessen pain and reduce itching. Use an over-the-counter pain medication to reduce discomfort. Pustules will form regardless of topical treatment. If pustules break, treat with a topical antibacterial ointment to prevent infection. Pustules may leave scars.

5 | Monitor symptoms.
Even a healthy adult may have a severe reaction to hundreds of stings, and people with certain allergies may develop serious complications. Watch for severe chest pain, nausea, severe sweating, loss of breath, severe swelling of limbs, and slurred speech. Seek immediate medical attention if any of these symptoms are present. In highly allergic people, anaphylaxis may occur from fire ant stings. Administer epinephrine immediately.

HOW TO AVOID A VAMPIRE ATTACK

1 Garlic, garlic, garlic.
Wear a necklace of strung garlic, which vampires despise. A hearty meal of pasta with garlic sauce and garlic bread will also help to ward them off. A garlic garland on a doorway will prevent a vampire from entering, even if he's been invited.

2 Stay outside during daylight hours.
While sunlight will not kill vampires, it will severely burn them. Most vampires sleep during daylight hours and avoid direct sunlight whenever possible, preferring to hunt for victims in the dark of night.

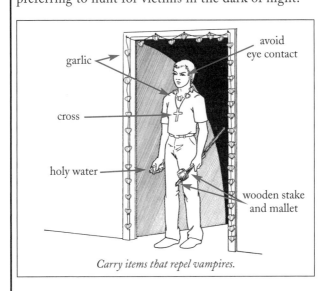

avoid eye contact

garlic

cross

holy water

wooden stake and mallet

Carry items that repel vampires.

3 Wear a cross.

Vampires dislike crosses, but a cross will not kill a vampire. Press the cross into the vampire's flesh to cause burning and scarring and drive the vampire away. For some vampires, the wearer must believe in the power of the cross for it to be an effective weapon.

4 Do not make direct eye contact.

To avoid the vampire's charms, do not look him directly in the eye.

5 Carry a vial of holy water.

Holy water thrown on a vampire causes severe burning and scarring. It may also be used as a detection device: The water will glow or bubble in the presence of the undead.

6 Carry a wooden stake.

For most vampires, a wooden stake driven through the heart causes death. The stake must be 2 to $2^1/_2$ feet long, with one end sharpened to a point and the other flat. Using a mallet, drive the stake in quickly with a single blow—a second blow may revive the vampire. The stake must pierce the heart and should be made of wood from an ash tree or a cross.

Be Aware

A vampire will bite any part of the body with ample blood flow. Major arteries are located in the throat, underarms, inner thighs, and at the back of ankles.

CHAPTER 2

ADVENTURE SPORTS

HOW TO BAIL OUT OF A STREET LUGE

1 Stay with your board.

Hold on to your board (even if it is broken), and use it to absorb some of the force of the impact. Do not reach out to grab passing objects or drag your legs to try to slow the luge, or you will risk serious injury. Keep your feet on the pegs and your hands on the handles with your back straight throughout the crash. Your helmet, full leathers, and pads will reduce road rash and also help to limit injury.

2 If you are separated from your luge, slide on your back, with your feet pointing downhill.

Do not roll. Rolling will result in more damage to your knees and elbows.

3 Slow your speed with your hands.

Move your arms to a 45 degree angle to your body. Place your gloved hands, palms down, on the road surface. Use the friction created by your gloves to slow your slide and control its direction. Adding pressure with your right hand will alter your slide path to the right, while pressure on your left hand will move you left. Expect to slide at least 200 feet (or triple that, if the road is wet) or until you hit an obstruction.

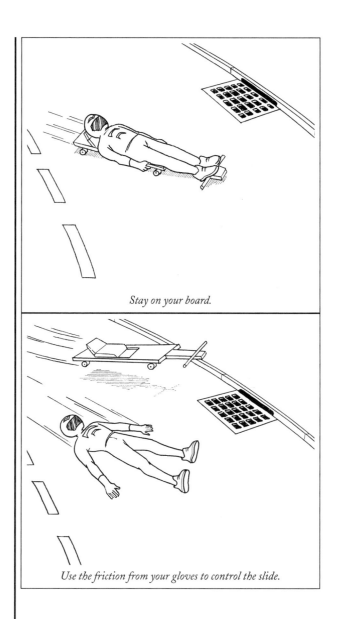

Stay on your board.

Use the friction from your gloves to control the slide.

4 Absorb the impact of the crash.

If an impact is unavoidable, bend your knees slightly to absorb the force of the crash feet first. Keep your toes pointed up, and hit the object with the balls of your feet, not your heels.

Be Aware

- A wheel coming off at speed is the most common street luge equipment failure.
- A truck that is too loose may not be noticeable until you are at speed, when severe wobbling will throw you from the board.
- Race luges do not have brakes.
- Spine, elbow, and knee pads are recommended to reduce serious injury.

HOW TO SURVIVE
A TWO-WAVE
HOLD-DOWN

A two-wave hold-down occurs when a surfer falls off a surfboard while riding a large wave and is held under water for two successive waves.

1 Bail your board.
If you are in the impact zone (the area where the lip of the wave meets the trough), dive off your board.

2 Avoid the "washing machine."
The washing machine, the white water that occurs as the wave crashes, is turbulent, full of air, and difficult to pierce and swim in. Attempting to surface through it will extend your hold-down.

3 Do not struggle.
Fighting a very big (or "rogue") wave will quickly exhaust you and increases your risk of drowning. Remember to "think before you sink."

4 Dive.
Swim as deep as you can. Big-wave leashes (the rope that connects you to your floating board) may be 20 feet long, allowing you to go very deep.

5 Allow the first wave to pass over you.

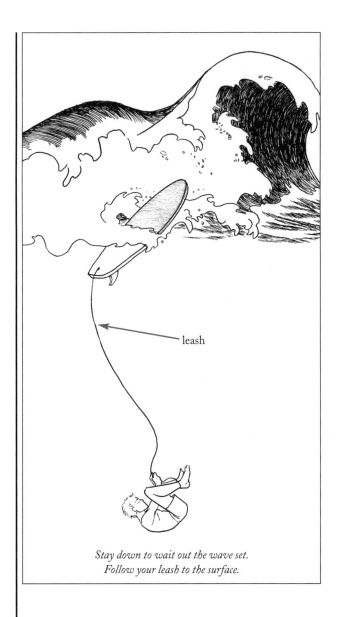

leash

Stay down to wait out the wave set.
Follow your leash to the surface.

6 Locate the board's leash.

If you are disoriented and unable to determine which way is up, grab your ankle and "follow your leash." Since the leash is attached to your floating surfboard, it will lead you to the surface.

7 Swim toward the surface.

As you approach the surface, place your hands above your head. Your surfboard may be "tombstoning," with its tail submerged and its nose pointing to the sky. Positioning your arms above your head will protect you from hitting your surfboard, a Jet Ski, or another wiped-out surfer as you come up for air.

8 Wait out the set of waves by diving underneath them.

Waves typically come in sets of three to five, depending on the day and surf conditions. Count the waves as they break so you'll know when the water will calm. Swim as deep as you can and curl your body into a defensive ball as the waves pass overhead. Come up for a quick breath between each wave, if possible, as you wait for the set to subside.

9 Paddle to calmer water.

When the set has passed, swim to the surface. Climb on your surfboard and paddle as fast as you can farther out to sea, beyond the impact zone, or into the "channel," the blue water that is sometimes to the left or right of the white water.

Be Aware

- Never position your surfboard between your body and a big wave: It will smash into you.
- Never put your back to the waves unless you are paddling to catch a wave and ride it.
- A big wave may hold you down for more than 30 seconds.

HOW TO LAND
A RUNAWAY HOT
AIR BALLOON

1 Use a radio to contact your chase crew.
A chase vehicle will be following your progress from
the ground, usually ready to meet the balloon when it
lands. Using the pilot's two-way radio, press the talk
button and explain your situation to the crew. Release
the button to listen. Tell a crew member to call emergency services to meet the balloon when it touches
down.

2 Establish whether the balloon is ascending or
descending.
Look to the horizon, 90 degrees to the right or left of
the direction the balloon is traveling. If the horizon is
moving higher, you are descending; if it is moving
lower, you are ascending.

3 Determine the balloon's farthest point of travel.
Face in the same direction the balloon is traveling.
Look for a point on the ground ahead of you that
does not appear to be rising or descending. This point
is the farthest the balloon will travel at its present rate
of descent. If no serious hazards (power lines, buildings, people) are between you and the farthest point
of travel, skip to step 5. If there are hazards ahead,
continue to step 4.

*The point on the ground ahead of you that is not rising
or falling is the balloon's farthest point of travel.*

4 Change your flight path.

To clear a populated area or avoid a collision, increase
the balloon's altitude by adding more heat to the
balloon. Locate the blast valve, a lever-type valve
protruding from under the propane burner. Open
the valve by rotating the handle to the vertical position, hold it open for 5 to 10 seconds, then release it.
(The valve is spring-loaded to the off position. The
faster you are descending, the longer you will need
to leave the valve open to slow your descent.) Leave
the valve closed for 10 seconds. Continue to operate
the valve in this sequence until you see the balloon
ascend. Do a horizon check (step 2) and check the
farthest point of travel (step 3) to determine your altitude and ability to clear obstructions.

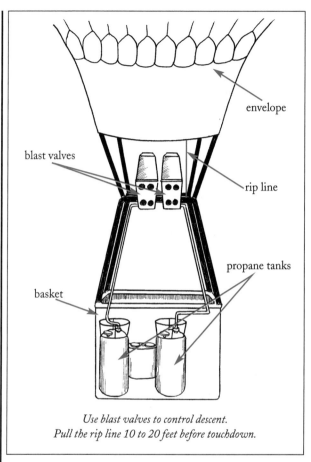

Use blast valves to control descent.
Pull the rip line 10 to 20 feet before touchdown.

5 Once all obstacles are cleared and a suitable landing
site is in view within your direction of travel, begin
your descent.

If you do not open the blast valve, the balloon will
slowly begin to descend. Hot air balloons are designed

so that terminal velocity (the speed at which the basket and balloon will hit the ground if the blast valve is fully closed) is only about 20 mph. At this speed, landing will be similar to landing under a parachute: a sharp bump, but survivable. Use the blast valve to slow your descent, if necessary, but be careful not to add so much hot air that you begin to ascend.

6 Pull the rip line.
The rip line is a red rope or strap hanging down into the basket from the envelope (the open balloon). It opens the vent at the top of the envelope, which allows hot air to escape quickly just before and right after landing. Ten to 20 feet before touchdown, pull hard on the rip line. There will be at least 20 feet of slack, perhaps more if the line is attached to pulleys to make pulling easier. Continue to pull the line until there is no more slack. Hold the line until the balloon has landed and deflated.

7 Brace for impact.
Bend your knees and grab the uprights or handles in the basket to avoid being thrown out upon contact with the ground. Avoid grabbing fuel lines or placing any part of your body outside the basket. Do not try to remain standing during impact: Collapse yourself into the bottom of the basket when you hit the ground.

8 Remain in the basket until the balloon has come to a complete stop.

The basket may bounce and skip several times before coming to a stop on the ground. The balloon should deflate and collapse in the downwind direction. If you have landed in trees, the basket should be upright, but you may need to wait for rescue.

Be Aware

- Failing to pull the rip line will result in a dangerous bouncing landing and increase the risk of the balloon hitting the ground and then floating away again.
- Though the envelope, wicker basket, and propane tanks will float, landing on water adds complications and should be considered only as a last resort.
- Hot air balloons have no mechanical steering mechanism—you can only force a balloon to climb (by opening the valve, adding propane to the envelope) or descend (by doing nothing). Steering is accomplished by harnessing wind currents at different altitudes.

HOW TO SURVIVE A BUNGEE JUMPING DISASTER

The bungee cord is under maximum stress at the very bottom of your jump, before you rebound; it is at this point that a break is most likely. If you are over water and the cord breaks or comes loose, you will be falling head first and have about two seconds to prepare for impact.

1 Straighten your legs and body.
Put your feet and legs together, and point your toes.

2 Tuck your chin into your chest as far as it will go.
Avoid the urge to look at the water rushing up to meet you: It will result in black eyes, whiplash, or severe spinal trauma.

3 Point your arms below your head in a diving position.
Ball your fists.

4 Enter the water fists first.
Your hands will break the surface tension of the water, putting less stress on your head. If the bungee cord was attached and broke at your rebound point, it will have slowed you almost to a stop, making for a relatively safe entry. If the cord was not attached or came loose during your fall, the impact will be more severe.

Enter the water fists first.

5 Spread your arms and legs.
After entering the water, spread your arms and legs to slow your momentum and reduce the possibility of hitting the bottom.

6 Swim to the surface.
Signal to the crew above that you are okay.

Be Aware

- Do not attempt to retie or hold the cord. You will not have time to tie a knot sufficient to support your weight, and the cord will fly out of your hands no matter how tightly you grasp it.
- Improper cord connection is a major source of bungee accidents. Before jumping, double-check that you are connected to the cord (generally with a carabiner) and the cord is connected to the bungee platform.
- Bungee cords are weight-specific, and you should always jump on a cord designed for your weight. Always overestimate, not underestimate, your weight.

HOW TO LAND A HANG GLIDER IN A WIND SHEAR

A wind gradient or "shear" is the boundary between two air masses moving at different velocities. The shear will stall the glider or produce extreme turbulence, making it difficult to control. Regain control by increasing speed, which will increase airflow across the sail (the flexible skin of the glider, also called the "wing").

1 Pull in on the control bar so the nose of the glider tilts toward the ground.

2 Shift your weight forward.
This will increase your velocity as you glide toward the ground.

3 Monitor your altitude.
Your variometer (a small computer strapped to the control bar) indicates your altitude in feet. You will probably be at a few thousand feet, descending quickly.

4 Monitor your airspeed.
Check the variometer for your speed. Your "VNE" (velocity never to exceed) on a hang glider is about 50 mph. If you are accelerating rapidly and approaching the glider's limits, pull back on the control bar slightly to bring the nose up and gain a bit more lift.

5 Unzip your harness.

As you approach an altitude of 500 feet, unzip your harness so you are no longer in the prone position. Your legs will be hanging down at a slight angle.

6 Position your hands on the down tubes.

As the glider approaches an altitude of 40 feet, move your hands from the horizontal section of the control bar to the down tubes, which are connected to either side of the bar.

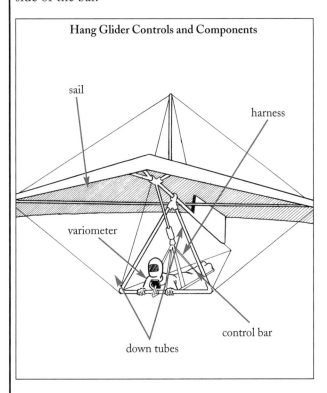

Hang Glider Controls and Components

sail

harness

variometer

control bar

down tubes

7 | Flare the sail.
Push the control bar forward with a smooth, fast motion. The hang glider's nose will pitch up. As the sail angle changes, the air between it and the ground will become compressed and act as an air brake to slow you down.

8 | Land in a standing position.
The glider will have slowed sufficiently to make a stand-up landing possible. As your feet touch the ground, begin a slow run to maintain control and keep the sail from pitching forward suddenly. If the glider frame has wheels, use them to absorb some of the force of the impact.

9 | Come to a stop.
The glider should settle gently to the ground.

Be Aware

- Many hang glider pilots wear a parachute on their chest to use if they are caught in dangerous turbulence or in a severe updraft that sends the glider above 10,000 feet.
- Carry a lightweight package of dental floss for use in an emergency, tree-based landing. When stuck in the tree, hold one end of the floss and toss the dispenser to rescuers. Instruct them to tie their end of the floss to a rope. Use the floss to pull the rope up, tie off, and climb down.

HOW TO CROSS BETWEEN BUILD-INGS ON A WIRE

A relatively level wire can be crossed by performing a modified Tyrolean traverse, a mountaineering technique used in crossing crevasses.

1 Test the wire.
The wire should be at least one inch thick and fully secured on both sides, preferably bolted or clamped (with steel) to stationary objects. Place your foot on the wire and apply hard downward pressure. The wire should flex slightly. If the wire remains taut, your weight will put too much stress on the side anchors.

2 Check the wire's angle.
The wire should be basically level, parallel to the ground. If slightly angled, the departure side should be a bit higher than the arrival side, so you are traveling "downhill" rather than "uphill" for at least the first half of the trip. (Because of the flex of the wire, you will be climbing "uphill" once you reach the midpoint of your journey.)

3 Protect your hands.
If you do not have gloves, tear out your pants pockets and use them as mittens, put your socks on your hands, or hold two squares of thick cardboard. Gloves

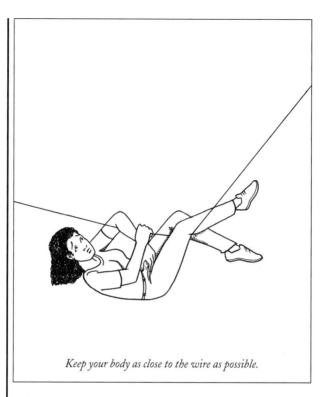

Keep your body as close to the wire as possible.

will protect your hands, absorb sweat, reduce friction and "rope burn," and allow your hands to slide more easily along the wire.

4 Hold the wire.

Stand on the edge of the building, facing the wire. Grab the wire with your hands, approximately two feet beyond the edge of the building. (Crouch down if the wire is at your feet.)

5 Position your legs.
Holding the rope tightly, bend at the waist and swing one leg up and over the wire. This leg should be on top of the wire, with the wire running under your knee. Swing your other leg up and cross your legs at your calves. The leg sitting on the wire should be "locked down" by your other leg.

6 Position your arms.
Holding on to the wire with your dominant hand, let go with your other hand and place your free arm up and over the wire. Bend this arm so the wire runs under your elbow, similar to the position of your leg. Your other arm should be gripping the wire a few inches beyond your bent elbow.

7 Check your position.
You should be hanging upside down, stomach toward the wire, head facing your direction of travel. Your body should be slightly bent at the elbows, knees, and waist.

8 Begin moving.
Slightly extend the arm that is gripping the wire. Pull your lower body after you, keeping one leg locked over the other. Your face should be as close to the wire as possible, with your hand not too far beyond your head. You will have moved about a foot.

9 Continue to face the wire, keeping your body as close to it as possible.
Do not look down.

10 Repeat.
Continue to travel in this fashion, resting between moves as necessary. Once you reach the midpoint of the wire, you will be traveling "uphill," and progress will be slower and more exhausting.

Be Aware

- Do not attempt to cross an electrical wire.
  Follow the path of the wire visually. If it appears to run from a pole into a building, the wire may be electrified and should not be crossed.
- A wire with too much flex will be extremely difficult to climb up once you reach its midpoint.

HOW TO STEER YOUR BIKE DOWN A ROCK FACE

A wrong turn can send your mountain bike down a sheer rock face.

1 Choose a line to follow.

The instant you feel the bike pitching forward down-slope, look ahead of you and choose the line that you will follow down the rock face. The line should be as free of large boulders, drop-offs, and deep ruts as possible. Follow this line.

2 Adjust your seating position.

Move slightly "out-of-saddle," above the seat with your knees bent, similar to a jockey on a horse running down the stretch. Keep your weight shifted toward the back of the saddle, or behind it, to counteract the pull of gravity.

3 Move the pedals to the three and nine o'clock positions.

Keep your feet on the pedals, with the pedals positioned across from one another. Do not put your feet straight up (twelve o'clock) and down (six o'clock), where the risk of making contact with rocks or the ground is greater. It is also more difficult to maintain a level position with the pedals straight up and down.

"out-of-saddle" position

elbows bent

knees bent

pedals at 3 and 9

Choose a line to follow down the rock face.

how to steer your bike down a rock face

4 Heavily apply the rear brake.

On most bikes, squeezing the brake lever by your right hand will apply the rear brake. Do so as you ride downslope to maintain control of the bike. If you do not brake sufficiently, you risk "bombing," or speeding out of control down the rock face. Apply the brakes enough to maintain a speed that enables you to see oncoming obstacles in your path.

5 Feather the front brake.

Using your left hand (on most bikes), gently apply the front brake as you climb obstacles, and release it to maintain momentum as you overcome them. This gentle apply-and-release action is called "feathering." Avoid applying the front brake suddenly and with full force or the bike will stop short and you will pitch over the handlebars.

6 Keep the bike in the middle-to-low gear range.

Low gears are easier to pedal; high gears are harder. The gear should be low enough that you can pedal easily over an obstacle, but not so low that you don't have any traction. It should not be so high that surmounting an obstacle becomes difficult or impossible.

7 Shift your weight.

As you approach large rocks and boulders, shift your body back to take the weight off the front wheel. This shift will allow the front wheel to more easily ride up and over the obstruction.

8 | Keep your knees and elbows bent.
Bend your knees and elbows to absorb shocks and to make fast, fluid position changes easier.

9 | Bail if you lose control.
If you feel yourself gaining sudden momentum and you begin to lose control, do not attempt to stay with the bike: You do not want to crash while riding at high speed. Let the bike drop out from beneath you, guiding it so it lands on the non-derailleur side to minimize damage that might make the bike unrideable. Tuck your elbows and knees in as you roll to safety.

HOW TO SURVIVE A MOTORCYCLE SPINOUT

1 Remain on the bike.

Try to regain control until the last possible moment. Even if you feel the bike begin to slide, the tires may regain traction in an instant, allowing you to recover and ride away. If the spinout is unavoidable, execute a low-side crash, wherein the bike slides out and away from you as you slide in the same direction, but behind the bike.

2 Apply both brakes.

As you feel the wheels lose traction, squeeze the brake lever with your right hand to apply the front brake, and press down on the pedal with your right foot to apply the rear brake. With both brakes locked, the bike will keep sliding out, eliminating the possibility of the wheels regaining traction and throwing you over the high side.

3 Slide.

Stay on your back as you slide, with your helmet slightly raised so you can see any approaching obstructions. Keep arms and legs slightly spread to distribute your body weight evenly and to reduce the possibility of a head-over-heels tumble.

4 Once you have come to a stop, stay still.
Do not try to stand up until your slide has stopped completely. You will pitch forward if you try to get up before your slide has completely stopped.

5 Get up slowly.
Check for injuries. If you were wearing full leathers, pads, gloves, and a helmet, you should be relatively uninjured.

6 Check the bike.
There is little chance of an explosion after a spinout, so it is safe to approach your motorcycle and look for damage.

Be Aware

- A high-side crash, in which the bike begins to slide in one direction, suddenly regains traction, and throws you across it in the opposite direction, is much more dangerous than a low-side crash and slide.
- Very few motorcycles have antilock brakes, so applying full braking is an effective way to lock the wheels and continue a low-side spinout.
- Motorcycles are highly sensitive to steering and brake application, and are not very forgiving. To avoid spinouts, always apply fast, smooth, gentle pressure and avoid jerky movements.

HOW TO SURVIVE A RACE CAR SPINOUT

On the racetrack, a high-speed (180 mph or more) spinout is a rear-wheel skid or slide, also called "oversteer." To counteract oversteer and regain control of the car, take the following steps.

1 Turn into the spinout.
Determine which way the rear of the car is sliding, then turn the steering wheel in the same direction. For example, if the back of the car is sliding to the right, turn the steering wheel to the right. Do not jerk the wheel. Apply smooth, controlled inputs or you risk losing control. (The steering systems on race cars vary, but typical stock cars have power-assisted steering.)

2 Apply steady throttle.
Oversteer occurs when the rear wheels lose traction. Because most race cars are rear-wheel driven, stepping on the gas and accelerating transfers the car's weight to the rear wheels, aiding traction. (These same forces "push" you back into the driver's seat when you accelerate quickly during everyday driving; this is called "weight transfer.")

3 Do not brake.
Applying the brakes transfers weight to the front wheels, which will only increase your spin.

Steer in the same direction as the skid.

4 Focus on the track ahead of you.

During the skid (and after you regain control), make sure the car is heading in the proper direction. Observe the cars around you and concentrate on where you want the car headed, not where it is going.

5 Unwind the wheel.

As you feel the rear of the car begin to come in line, slowly bring the steering wheel back to center. Avoid attempting to "counteract" the spin by turning the wheel too far in the opposite direction. If you cannot regain control, continue to the next step.

how to survive a race car spinout

6 Brake.

Once the car is out of control and a crash is imminent, apply the brakes to slow your rotational momentum.

7 Prepare for impact.

A stock car has a full race cage, a racing harness (a five-point seat belt), and a collapsible steering column, and you will be wearing a head and neck restraint. If you sense that impact with the wall or another vehicle is imminent, relax your body and let the car's safety devices protect you. Loosen your grip on the wheel or let go of it, keep your knees slightly bent, and do not tense your neck muscles.

8 Get out.

Your fire-protection suit and gloves are designed to protect you from heat and flames for several minutes. However, in the event of fire, get out of the car (climb through the window opening) as soon as it is safe to do so, or when help arrives.

Be Aware

• Do not downshift during a spinout—it is likely to lock the rear wheels. Downshift only when the car is moving in a straight line.

• Stock cars do not have air bags.

• All stock cars have braided, stainless-steel fuel lines to reduce the possibility of a fuel spill after a crash.

- The fuel tank in a stock car contains a rubber "bladder" filled with foam to absorb crash impact forces and reduce the chance of explosion.
- Standard racing tires (or "racing slicks") have no treads. The fewer the grooves, the more rubber the tire has against the road to increase traction. After multiple laps (the number varies with the tire compound and track conditions) tires get too hot, their rubber compounds break down, and they need to be replaced.
- During a race, the car's cockpit temperature may reach 130 degrees Fahrenheit or more, and the steel roll cage may be even hotter.

HOW TO SURVIVE WHEN STUCK ON A MOUNTAIN LEDGE IN A BLIZZARD

⭐ Check the mountain above you.
If the rock face above your ledge is vertical or nearly vertical, snow will probably not build up sufficiently to create a serious danger of a slide or avalanche. If the angle of incline allows snow to build up, however, prepare for sliding snow that has accumulated above. Stay as far back from the edge as possible.

⭐ Make a guardrail.
Using snow and any available loose rocks, make a large, horizontal mound at the edge of the ledge. This "guardrail" may prevent you from accidentally rolling off if you fall asleep.

⭐ Build shelter.
Use a tent, tarp, or bivouac sack to make a windbreak and to prevent snow from accumulating on your ledge and burying you. Secure the material to the rock face using anchors and rope, or with rocks and snow on the edges. If space permits, build a snow cave by making a large pile of snow and hollowing it out. Position the entrance so it faces the mountain, not the open air, if there is room to do so.

✪ Anchor yourself to the ledge.

Use anchors and rope to secure yourself to the rock face. Run the rope through the anchor and tie it tightly around your waist. If anchors are not available, make a loop with the rope and place it over a rock outcropping or a large boulder. The loop should be positioned so that if you fall, it slips further down the outcropping or boulder, rather than off it. Tie a knot in the rope just beyond the loop, then tie the remaining portion of the rope tightly around your waist.

✪ Stay warm.

Put on all available clothing, especially a hat, mittens or gloves, dry socks, and shoes. To reduce heat loss, use any extra clothing as padding and insulation. Place it under you so it acts as a barrier between your body and the snow or rock you are lying on.

✪ Eat and drink.

If you do not have water to drink, use a small camping stove to melt snow into drinkable water and to cook any available food. When using the stove in a snow cave, poke a hole in the roof to allow carbon monoxide to escape.

✪ Massage and exercise.

To keep blood circulating and prevent frostbite, massage your hands, fingers, toes, nose, and ears. Muscle activity generates heat, so periodically do push-ups, sit-ups, or just tense and relax muscles to maintain adequate circulation and stay warm.

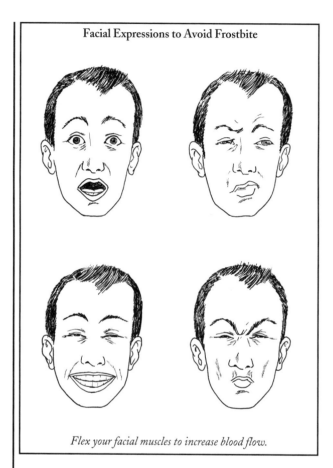

Facial Expressions to Avoid Frostbite

Flex your facial muscles to increase blood flow.

 Wait.

Do not attempt to leave your ledge until the snow has stopped and winds have calmed sufficiently. Most blizzards last a day or two at most, with three days possible but unlikely.

HOW TO SKI OFF
A 100-FOOT DROP

1 Look for danger below.
Just before you ski off the edge of the cliff, look down
and out over the slope. If your projected path takes
you toward rocks, trees, or another cliff, change your
takeoff angle by jumping to the left or right so you
will head toward safer, wide-open terrain.

2 Jump up and off the ledge.
Just as you are leaving the ground, hop up and slightly
forward to help you clear any rocks or other obstructions that may be hidden just below the ledge and that
could knock you off balance.

3 Pull your legs and skis up and tuck them under your
rear end.
This compressed "ball" position will help you maintain balance while airborne and help you to land
safely.

4 Thrust both arms out in front of you, elbows
slightly bent.
Avoid the "cat out the window" position, where your
arms and hands are splayed out above your head. That
position will put you off balance when you land.

arms out front

elbows bent

legs and skis tucked in

Land on steep terrain to minimize injury.

5 | Look out, not down.
Looking down at the ground will lead to a "door hinge" landing, where you bend forward at the waist and plant your face in the slope. Look out over the mountain.

6 | Focus on a suitable landing site.
Land on very steep terrain. Avoid a low-angled slope or, worse, a flat section of the mountain. As long as the snow is powder and at least one foot deep, you should be able to land without serious injury.

7 | Bend your knees as you land.
As you approach the side of the mountain, keep your knees bent to absorb the force of the impact with the ground. Avoid leaning back, which will cause a "tail first" landing and probable back injury. If you cannot ski away from a landing, land on your hip. Do not lean too far forward or you will fall on your face.

8 | Extend your feet, bend your knees, and turn across (or "into") the mountain to slow down.
Because of your extreme speed while airborne, you must minimize acceleration by turning as soon as you land, or you risk hurtling down the mountain out of control. Modern skis should stay on top of deep powder instead of sinking, giving you a reasonable amount of control.

9 Continue making turns to keep control and reduce speed as you ski away.

Be Aware

- If you feel yourself falling backward while airborne, move your hands further in front of you and make fast circular motions, forward and back. This balancing maneuver is called "rolling down the windows."

- In any jump greater than 15 feet, avoid landing in the same spot a previous jumper landed; the snow will already be compacted and will not provide sufficient cushioning.

CHAPTER 3

EXTREME SITUATIONS

HOW TO SURVIVE NUCLEAR FALLOUT

1 Put distance between yourself and the blast site.
Radioactivity diminishes significantly with physical protection, time, and distance from the epicenter of the explosion. For a five-megaton weapon detonated at 2,000 feet (an average weapon yield and detonation altitude), move at least 20 miles away for safety. Travel in a crosswind direction (not with or against the wind) as quickly as possible. Drive a car with the windows rolled up. If no car is available, ride a bike or run.

2 Find shelter.
Any material will at least partially block radioactive particles. However, equal thickness, dense materials like lead, concrete, and steel are more effective than porous materials like wood, tile, drywall, and insulation. If you cannot get into a designated fallout shelter, move to the basement of a building made of stone or concrete, preferably with few windows. The deeper the basement, the more protection you'll have from radioactive particles.

3 Gather water.
The existing water in a basement water tank should be safe to drink, as is water in pipes. However, if dams and water treatment plants become contaminated, new water entering the system may be dangerous. Stored bottled water is safe, provided the water does

not come into contact with the outside of the bottle, which may be covered with radioactive particles.

4 Gather food.

Packaged foods and those that can be peeled or shelled—and that are already in the house—are safe to eat, provided the packages, peels, or shells are rinsed thoroughly with clean water to eliminate radioactive alpha and beta particles. Canned goods are also safe, provided the cans are washed with clean water and food does not come into contact with the can's exterior. Avoid foods from opened packages, even if the packages have been resealed with tape or clips.

5 Wash your hands before eating and drinking.

Using soap and clean water, wash your hands (and under your fingernails) thoroughly before handling food. Radioactive particles traveling on dust can be transferred to food easily. Once ingested, these may settle in bone marrow and internal organs, causing long-term illness.

6 Stay in your shelter.

Without a radiation rate meter, you will not know when it is safe to leave your shelter. If you have access to a battery-powered radio, listen for news and monitor emergency announcements regarding the safety of your location. Cellular and wired telephones may not work, and even satellite phones may suffer from severe interference. If available, use a CB or short-wave radio to communicate with others until telephone service is restored.

Be Aware
A radiation suit will prevent you from tracking radioactive particles into the shelter (as long as you remove the suit upon entering), but will not offer protection from fallout.

What to Do If You Think You Have Been Exposed to Fallout

1 Remove contaminated clothing.
Radioactive dirt and dust will cling to clothing, causing radiation burns, sickness, and contamination of other people and objects. Remove contaminated clothing before entering a clean area.

2 Take a shower.
Showering in clean, fresh water is the best way to remove harmful radioactive particles from your skin. Use soap and warm water and clean under fingernails and toenails. If you do not have a sufficient amount of uncontaminated water for a shower, fill a bucket with as much water as possible and take a sponge bath, making sure the contaminated water goes down the drain.

3 Take potassium iodide (KI) or potassium iodate (KIO₃) pills.

Potassium iodide or iodate helps prevent radiation absorption by the thyroid gland. While it is most effective when taken 48 hours prior to exposure, potassium iodide provides some benefit if taken within 16 hours of exposure to radioactive fallout. If no pills are available, mix 2 ounces of granulated potassium iodide (available at chemical supply stores) with clean water and shake or stir vigorously, adding more potassium iodide until the solution is fully saturated. (You will see unmixed granules at the bottom of the glass or bottle.) Take 4 drops of the solution per day for at least 10 days. For infants, paint iodine onto the soles of the feet.

4 Monitor your symptoms.

Mild exposure to radiation may result in skin burns, weakness, loss of appetite, vomiting, and diarrhea, while higher doses lead to fainting, bleeding from the nose and gums, hair loss, anemia, hemorrhage, brain damage, and sometimes death within 48 hours. In general, breathing or swallowing radioactive particles or exposure to gamma rays result in more severe illness than surface exposure to radioactive particles, which are relatively easy to remove from the skin.

5 Get help.

Though there is no known treatment for radiation sickness, seek medical attention as soon as it is safe and possible to do so. A bone marrow transplant might alleviate some damage from exposure.

Be Aware

- Iodized salt is not an effective protection against radiation damage to the thyroid: You will get salt poisoning before absorbing enough iodine to have a beneficial effect.
- Victims of exposure to high levels of radiation may appear to improve several days after exposure as the body superficially heals. But deep biological damage remains, and the victim may rapidly deteriorate after the initial improvement.

HOW TO CLEAN AND COOK A SQUIRREL

1 Place the squirrel on the ground, belly up.

2 Pull the end of the squirrel's tail up slightly toward you.

3 Cut.
Using a very sharp knife, make a small incision across the base of the tail, where it meets the body. Do not cut the tail completely off: The cut should be deep enough to sever the tail but should leave the skin on top of the squirrel intact.

4 Split the hide.
Make an incision through the hide down the inside of one hind leg so it connects to the cut at the tail. Repeat for the other hind leg. You should have one continuous incision from the tip of one hind leg to the tail, then back up the other hind leg.

5 Place your foot on the squirrel's tail.

6 Pull.
Pull up sharply on the squirrel's hind legs. The skin should peel off from the bottom of the squirrel to the head. Squirrels have tough skin that is difficult to remove, so it will take some time.

7 Remove the head and feet.
Cut the squirrel's head off at the neck, then cut off the feet.

8 Field dress.
Slice the belly from stem to stern and remove all entrails. Discard. Rinse off excess blood with clean water.

9 Cook.
A smaller, younger squirrel will be tender and may be roasted, while an older squirrel will have tough meat that is better stewed, if a pot is available.

- **To ROAST.** For a youngster, sharpen a green stick (sapling) and impale the squirrel from stem to stern. Lay the sapling horizontally between two upright, forked branches positioned on either side of a fire. Slowly cook the squirrel, rotating the sapling periodically for even cooking. The meat is done when it is slightly pink inside the thickest part of the thigh. Cut with your knife to check.

- **To STEW.** Cut an older squirrel into serving pieces: legs, back, and rib sections. Place the sections in a pot of boiling water. Add fuel to the fire to return the pot to a boil, then remove fuel as necessary to maintain a simmer. The squirrel is done when the meat falls off the bone easily. Remove from the heat and remove bones before eating.

HOW TO DEAL WITH A SUSPICIOUS WHITE POWDER

⭐ Hold your breath.
As soon as you see suspicious white powder, stop inhaling. Anthrax spores are generally only fatal when inhaled in large numbers.

⭐ Do not crouch to the floor.
Unless aerosolized as a bioweapon, anthrax spores fall to the ground and stay there when released. Stand on a table or chair when handling the envelope or other container of the spores to reduce the chance of inhalation—when the spores fall to the floor, you'll be farther from them.

⭐ Stay upwind of the letter or parcel.
Anthrax spores travel on wind gusts. Hold the envelope or other container away from you and downwind of any air vents or room fans. If outside, leave the envelope in place and get inside. Close all windows and doors.

⭐ Cover your nose and mouth.
For the best protection, wear a gas mask capable of filtering particles 1 to 5 microns in size. If no gas mask is available, use a surgical mask or a bandanna to cover your nose and mouth.

hold breath

Stay above and upwind of a suspicious white powder.

⭐ Do not wash clothes or disinfect surfaces.
Detergents may increase the virulence of anthrax spores.

⭐ Call the authorities to report the incident.

Be Aware

- Anthrax cannot be transmitted from person to person, so it is safe to warn people around you of the danger.
- Anthrax spores may cause localized infection if they enter the body through the skin, especially through a cut. Wear rubber gloves when handling a suspect letter or parcel.

HOW TO SURVIVE IF YOUR FOOD IS BEING POISONED

1 Induce vomiting.
Regurgitating the agent before it can be absorbed into the bloodstream will help to reduce its effects. If you cannot force yourself to vomit, take 1 tablespoon of syrup of ipecac, followed by a glass of water, soda, or juice. (Do not drink milk.) Vomiting should occur within a few minutes. If it does not, follow with a second tablespoon of the ipecac.

2 Take activated charcoal.
Drink a single, premixed container of activated charcoal slurry, or mix the powder with the proper amount of liquid (follow the instructions on the package) to absorb the poison. Do not take activated charcoal within 30 minutes of taking ipecac, or while vomiting is still occurring. Activated charcoal is most effective when administered in an emergency room.

3 Test food and drink promptly.
Take your meal to a lab and have it tested. Once the toxins are identified, an antidote, if available, and treatment can be administered. However, some exotic poisons such as dioxin, mercury, and other heavy metals may be difficult or impossible to detect, especially in low concentrations.

4 Seek medical attention promptly.

Call the local poison control center as soon as possible. Some remedies can be prescribed over the phone, without an examination. With an examination and blood, urine, and other tests, health-care professionals can determine the effects of the poison on your body.

Be Aware

- Poisons may be sedatives (or mixed with sedatives) to induce loss of consciousness. If you pass out but wake up later, do not assume the poison has worked its way out of your system.
- A percolating drink—or one that appears to be foaming or releasing quantities of odd-smelling gas—should be avoided. The chemical agent phosgene, for example, is an odorous poisonous gas at room temperature but may be a liquid when cooled.
- Depending on the agent, poison may be absorbed into the bloodstream in seconds or minutes.

In sufficient concentrations, several common poison agents are relatively easy to detect in food or drink, based on their odor. These include:

ARSINE
Type: blood agent
Odor: garlic
Timing of Symptoms: minutes or hours
Symptoms: may include headache, dizziness, difficulty breathing, abdominal pain, nausea, vomiting, and bloody urine

Chlorine
Type: choking agent
Odor: bleach
Timing of Symptoms: seconds to minutes
Symptoms: may include headache, nausea, weakness, and loss of consciousness (when ingested in high doses)

Cyanide
Type: choking agent
Odor: bitter almonds
Timing of Symptoms: seconds to minutes
Symptoms: may include headache, nausea, weakness, anxiety, and loss of consciousness

Hydrogen Chloride
Type: blood agent
Odor: acrid, metallic
Timing of Symptoms: seconds to minutes
Symptoms: may include eye and skin irritation, fluid in the lungs, and blue skin (in high doses)

Phosgene
Type: choking agent
Odor: decaying fruit
Timing of Symptoms: 1 to 24 hours
Symptoms: may include burning eyes, sore throat, cough, and chest tightness

HOW TO TAKE
A BULLET

1 Face the shooter.
You do not want to take the bullet in your back or the base of your skull.

2 Get low.
In addition to making yourself a smaller target, by keeping a low profile you will be better able to protect your head, neck, and midline—all areas where a bullet wound is most likely to cause fatal injury or permanent disability.

3 Sit.
Sit with your rear end on the ground. Bend your knees and keep your legs in front of you, protecting your midline with your shins and thighs.

4 Move your elbows into the center of your body.
Place both forearms in front of you, covering your face.

5 Place your hands over your head.
Hold your fingers together, with your palms toward you. Keep your hands an inch or two in front of you to absorb the impact of the bullet.

6 Wait for the impact.
You may notice little more than a "punch" sensation, or you may feel nothing at all.

7 Determine the site of the injury.

Bullet wounds in the hands and feet, lower legs, and forearms are rarely fatal, provided blood loss is controlled.

8 Control the bleeding.

Place firm, direct pressure on the wound to slow blood loss. If the bullet entered an appendage and pressure does not stop the bleeding, use a belt or narrow strip of cloth as a tourniquet. Place the tourniquet on the affected limb, several inches above the injury site. It should be tight enough to stop heavy blood flow. A tourniquet may cause permanent damage to the affected limb, and should be used only as a last resort. Never leave a tourniquet in place for more than a few minutes.

9 Get help.

Seek medical attention as soon as possible.

Be Aware

- If you are crouching next to a wall, stay a foot or more away from the surface. Bullets will skid along the wall after impact.
- Gunshot wounds to the neck are almost always fatal.
- Most interior walls and doors (including car doors) will not stop a bullet larger than .22 or .25 caliber.

HOW TO SURVIVE IF YOU ARE BURIED ALIVE

1 Conserve your air supply.

If you are buried in a typical coffin, you will have enough air to survive for an hour or two at most. Take deep breaths, then hold for as long as possible before exhaling. Do not breathe and then swallow, which will lead to hyperventilation. Do not light a match or lighter. Combustion will quickly use your available oxygen. It is safe to use a flashlight if you have one. Do not yell. Yelling will lead to panic, which will increase your heart rate and lead to fast breathing that will rapidly consume your air supply.

2 Press up on the coffin lid with your hands.

An inexpensive "pine box" (chipboard coffin) or a recycled paperboard coffin will have some give to it, so it will be relatively easy to break through. If you feel flex in the coffin lid, continue to step 3. A metal-clad or hardwood coffin will be impossible to pierce. In this case, your only hope is to signal for rescue. Use a metal object (ring, belt buckle, coin, flask, pen) to signal that you are alive. Tap SOS, the international distress signal, on the coffin lid: three quick taps, followed by three slower taps, followed by three quick taps. Continue to repeat the distress call until someone hears you.

3 Remove your shirt.

Cross your arms over your chest, then uncross your arms so that your elbows are bent and your hands are at your shoulders. Pull your shirt up and off your head from the shoulders, do a partial sit-up (as much as you can in the space available), then pull your shirt over your head and off.

4 Tie the bottom of the shirt in a knot.

The shirt should have only one large opening, at the neck, as does a bag.

5 Place your head through the neck hole.

The knot should be on the top of your head. The shirt will prevent you from suffocating on loose earth.

6 Break through the coffin.

Using your feet, begin kicking the coffin lid. A cheap coffin may have already split from the weight of the earth above, making your job easier. Break apart the lid with your hands and feet and let the loose dirt rush in.

7 Use your hands to push the dirt toward your feet.

There should be some space at the bottom end of the coffin, below your feet. As the dirt rushes in, work quickly but calmly to fill the space at your feet. When this space fills up, push dirt to your sides. Breathe slowly and regularly.

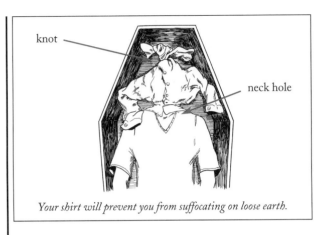

knot

neck hole

Your shirt will prevent you from suffocating on loose earth.

8 Sit up.

As you move to a seated position, the loose earth above will move to fill the space you just occupied. As the dirt falls, continue to push it into the coffin until you can stand up.

9 Stand.

Once you are standing, you should be able to push the dirt above you up and out of the grave. When you have cleared all the dirt above you, climb out.

Be Aware

- A recently interred coffin will be covered with loose earth that is relatively easy to dig through.
- Escaping from a coffin interred during a rain storm will be difficult. The compacted weight of the wet earth will make digging almost impossible.
- The higher the clay content of the soil, the more difficult your escape will be.

HOW TO DRIVE THROUGH A CHEMICAL SPILL

1 Extinguish any cigarettes.
Many hazardous chemicals are highly combustible. If you are smoking, put the cigarette out completely in your ashtray. Make sure all embers are fully extinguished. Do not throw a lit cigarette out the window.

2 Turn off the air circulation systems.
Make sure the heat, air-conditioning, and all blower fans are off and vents are closed. These systems will bring contaminated outside air into the car.

3 Shut the windows.
Make sure all windows (and the sunroof, if you have one) are fully closed.

4 Cover your mouth.
Tie a handkerchief, cloth napkin, or bandanna around your head so the fabric covers your nose and mouth. Do not wet the fabric beforehand: Some gases and vapors are attracted to water and may combine with it to form dangerous and/or unstable compounds.

5 Monitor your speed.
In most cases, you should drive though chemical hazards at a moderate speed. However, when driving
through a dry chemical spill, move extremely slowly
(less than 15 mph) to avoid kicking up plumes of
toxic dust.

6 Drive uphill and upwind of the spill site.
Once through the spill, continue driving away from
it. Many dangerous gases are heavier than air and will
tend to settle in low-lying areas. Get to a higher elevation immediately.

7 Abandon your car.
When you are uphill and upwind of the spill, at least
half a mile away, and in an unpopulated and low-
traffic area, leave your car, which is now contaminated. Use caution when getting out, and do not
touch any external surface.

8 Run.
Proceed uphill and upwind of your car as quickly as
possible. Do not crawl.

9 Inform authorities that your vehicle and possibly
your person are contaminated.

Be Aware

- It is always safer to turn around and drive away from a spill rather than through it. Do not drive through a spill unless you are instructed to do so, or have no other choice.
- HEPA and other microfilters used in the air circulation systems of some cars are not effective protection from toxic substances.

Chapter 4

ON THE MOVE

HOW TO SURVIVE A ROLLOVER IN A CAR

1 Use your legs to brace your lower body.
You will have just fractions of a second to prepare for impact. Remove your feet from the pedals, placing the soles of your feet flat against the sheet metal behind the pedals. Using your leg muscles, press hard against the metal surface, as if you are on a leg press. Extend your legs as far as possible, pressing your body back into the seat.

2 Push your upper body against the seat.
Using both hands, grab the wheel at the three and nine o'clock positions and grip tightly. Push out with your arms, pressing your torso as far into the seat back as possible. Keep your elbows tucked in to your body.

3 Secure your head and neck.
Press the back of your head and neck into the headrest as far as they will go.

4 Tense all of your muscles.
Exert as much force as possible to move your entire body back into the seat, which is your best protection during the rollover.

chapter 4: on the move

Tense your muscles and force your body back into the seat.

5   If the car lands upright and the engine is still running, steer the car away from obstructions or oncoming traffic.
Because they have a lower center of gravity than trucks and SUVs, cars tend to roll over completely and land on their wheels.

6   If the car lands on its roof, turn off the ignition.
Most modern cars (those manufactured after 1985) have a cutoff switch that kicks in automatically to stop fuel flow to the engine when the vehicle senses a rollover. If the engine is still running, turn it off.

7   Carefully remove your seat belt.
You will be hanging upside down, with your safety belt holding you in your seat. Brace your hands and feet against the roof before unlatching the belt.

In a single-vehicle rollover with no collision, your primary (steering wheel) air bag may not have deployed. Any side curtain air bags and head protection systems will have deployed, however, so watch for hot gas escaping from these devices.

8 Escape from the car.
The vehicle's steel safety cage and roll bars may have preserved the integrity of the car, keeping the doors in working condition. If you cannot open the door, crawl through the window. If the window has not been broken during the rollover and is intact, try to roll it down. If you are unable to do so, use a metal object such as a steering wheel lock to break the glass.

9 Run.
Move away from the car as quickly as possible in case there is a fuel leak, which could cause an explosion.

Be Aware

- SUVs and trucks have less-stringent safety standards than cars and tend to have a higher center of gravity, making them more prone to a rollover.
- The roofs of early-model SUVs and trucks may be deformed in a rollover.
- When occupants are wearing seat belts during a rollover, most injuries are to the head (from hitting the roof supports) and arms (from being flung out the windows by rollover forces). When occupants are not wearing seat belts, they will most likely be thrown from the vehicle.

HOW TO DEAL WITH A QUADRUPLE BLOWOUT

1 Hold steering wheel firmly.
Though the car will become increasingly difficult to control, concentrate on keeping the car moving in a straight line. Grasp the steering wheel tightly—it will be shaking violently.

2 Put your hazard lights on.
Your hazards will signal drivers behind you that you are in distress.

3 Apply the brakes.
Put light but steady pressure on the brake pedal to reduce speed. Though the tires are blown, you should still have some tread remaining on each wheel for a few minutes. The "contact patches" (the section of each tire in contact with the road surface) will be greatly reduced, however, and will continue to shrink as pieces of the tire spin off the wheel. The smaller the contact patch, the less friction available to the brakes, less stopping power, and more possibility of spinning out of control. The car will be shaking, along with the steering wheel, and the vehicle will become progressively harder to control.

4 Steer toward a safe stopping point.

Scan the road ahead. Look for a relatively open, flat area on the shoulder. If you are in the center or inside lane, signal and move to the outer lane, but make a gradual lane change with no sudden inputs to the steering wheel. If you cannot see or cannot immediately reach a stopping point, see "How to Continue Driving on Four Blown Tires," below.

5 Let the car roll to a stop.

Once you reach a safe area out of the flow of traffic, take your foot off the brake and allow the car to coast to a stop.

How to Continue Driving on Four Blown Tires

1 Go straight.

If you are on a bridge or stretch of road where you cannot stop safely, keep the car moving in a straight line for as long as possible. Driving on four blown tires, and, eventually, four rims, will be similar to driving on ice: You will have very little stopping power, and the car will tend to spin as you enter turns.

2 Accelerate smoothly.

Less friction with the road surface increases the likelihood of spinning wheels, which will make fast acceleration impossible. Apply the throttle (gas pedal) smoothly and sparingly and only to maintain control while moving in a straight line or through a very

Stay on the roadway at all costs.

gradual turn. Most front-wheel-drive cars have an open differential, where the wheel with the least resistance gets the power. As the tires disintegrate, the wheel with less friction will spin, and the car will swerve from side to side.

3 Stay on a paved surface.
Avoid driving the car off the roadway at all costs. With no rubber remaining, the metal wheels will readily bite into soft ground and cause the car to flip.

4 Listen for the last pieces of rubber to fly off the wheels.

The car will shake increasingly violently as the tires disintegrate, and you will hear very loud flapping sounds from the corners. The tread will not stay centered on the wheel, and the contact patch will shift wildly, making the car difficult to control. After a mile or two, the last pieces of rubber will come off, and the flapping sound will disappear. Provided the shredded tires have not gotten caught in the wheel wells, driving on the metal rims should provide less shaking and more control. Your contact area with the road, however, will be extremely small (the width of two pencils for each wheel) and traction will be severely limited. The rims will spark as you drive on them.

5 Pull over as soon as possible.

Eventually, the rims will flatten or crack and the bottom of the car will begin dragging on the road until the friction stops your progress. Steel wheels will last longer and go further than aluminum or magnesium wheels, which are lighter, more brittle, and have a tendency to bend and break under stress.

Be Aware

Run-flat tires have reinforced sidewalls that will support the weight of the car and allow driving with a puncture. However, tires that are severely punctured by treadles or road spikes will begin to shred, and the sidewalls will eventually separate from the tread and come off.

HOW TO SURVIVE IF YOUR CAR CAREENS DOWN A MOUNTAINSIDE

1 Apply firm and steady braking pressure.

Do not slam on the brakes as you leave the roadway and begin traveling down the slope. If you lock up your brakes, the wheels lose traction and may cause the vehicle to skid sideways, increasing the risk of a rollover.

2 Maintain a firm grip on the steering wheel.

The car is likely to bounce wildly and severely jostle you in your seat. Place your hands at the ten and two o'clock positions. Keep your thumbs outside the steering wheel: If the car hits an object, the force may yank the steering wheel around, injuring your thumbs or arms.

3 Point the car downhill.

Keep the car facing and traveling straight downhill, continuing to apply steady braking pressure. A vehicle is much more likely to roll over if it is sideways across a hill. Though you may be able to survive a rollover, you will have no control and will not be able to stop the car.

4 Steer.

Keep the front wheels turned in the direction the car is sliding/moving in order to increase traction and make braking and steering more effective.

5 Downshift.

Once you regain control of the car and it is facing downhill, use engine braking to slow the car's momentum. If the car has a manual transmission, keep your foot off the gas and downshift to first gear. For an automatic, keep your foot off the gas and shift the car from drive to first gear or the lowest gear available. Continue to apply just enough braking pressure to control your speed, but not enough to lock up your wheels.

6 Turn the wheel in the same direction the car is sliding to regain control.

On a steep downslope, the weight of the car will transfer to the front axle as you brake, possibly causing the tail to spin out and around toward the front. To regain traction, turn the wheel in the direction the vehicle is sliding, then apply the gas lightly.

7 Use steady braking pressure to stop the car.

Once the car has stopped moving, apply the emergency brake and get out. If you cannot stop the car using the brakes, go to step 8.

Ram an obstacle only as a last resort.

8 Attempt to "high-center" the car.

If you are not able to stop the car in time to avoid an approaching cliff, look for a large rock or fallen tree. Drive over the object centered between your front wheels to try to force the car to "bottom out" and get stuck before the rear wheels roll over the obstacle. This maneuver will typically work only with an obstacle that is about one foot high. If you cannot high-center the car, continue to the next step.

9 Ram an obstacle.

Slow the car to 20 mph or less to increase your chance of survival. Ram the car head on into a tree or large

how to survive if your car careens down a mountainside

boulder to stop your progress. Do not turn the car across the slope and ram the object sideways; you risk a rollover. You (and all passengers) must be wearing a seat belt and the car must have an air bag for you and your front-seat passenger. Ram the obstacle only as a last resort.

Be Aware
A vehicle's antilock braking system is usually not effective off-road: ABSs monitor wheel speed, and will apply the brakes only enough to equalize the rotation of the wheels, not to stop them from spinning when there is no traction. You will need to pump the brakes and to be aware that the braking system might apply pressure unequally to the wheels.

How to Get the Car Back to the Road

1 Assess damage to vehicle.
Once you have stopped the car, get out and inspect the vehicle. Check for brake fluid (red liquid pooling under the car) or damaged steering components (broken rods hanging down from the insides of the front wheels). Do not drive the car if it has a broken axle or damaged steering components, or if it is leaking brake fluid.

2 Walk your intended route before driving it.
Look for ditches, obstacles, and cliffs that may prevent you from getting back to the roadway.

3 | Drive slowly.
Use light acceleration and braking and smooth steering. Keep your speed to 5 mph or less, terrain permitting. Follow the off-roading maxim: "As slow as you can, as fast as you must."

4 | Monitor the path in front of you.
Look downslope to determine where you are headed and when you will need to stop the car. On a mountainside, the car will require 10 to 20 times its normal dry-pavement stopping distance.

5 | Look for a switchback.
Most steep mountain roads contain numerous switchbacks, or sharp turns that take you across the slope but at a slightly higher or lower elevation (depending on your direction of travel). If you see a lower section of the road cutting across the mountainside ahead of you, attempt to steer the car back onto the asphalt at the next opportunity. Watch for steep drop-offs that are common in mountain road cuts, however.

Be Aware

- Most passenger cars will roll side over side on any slope greater than 30 degrees.
- When your air bag deploys, fuel to the engine will likely be cut off, making further controlled driving impossible.

HOW TO SURVIVE WHEN STUCK ON AN OPENING DRAWBRIDGE

1 Draw attention to yourself.

Two-leaf bascule drawbridges—those with two movable sections of roadway that swing from horizontal to vertical—will have a bridge "tender" (operator) in the control house who should be able to stop the opening. Flash your headlights and honk your horn repeatedly to attract his attention so he will lower the drawbridge. If the bridge tender cannot see you (his view may be blocked by one of the open spans) or is not paying attention, you will have to proceed on your own.

2 Back up.

Drawbridges take several minutes to open fully. If the opening span is still relatively horizontal, back up off the bridge (or at least as far back as you can).

3 Get out.

Place your car in gear (or in park if it has an automatic transmission) and apply the emergency brake. Get out of the car and move away: Even with the brake on, the vehicle will begin sliding backward by the time the roadway opens about 30 degrees.

4 Hold on.

The bridge should have some type of railing and/or a grated road surface that offers hand- and footholds. If a railing is present, grab one of the vertical (fast becoming horizontal) railing supports. Wrap both your arms around the section and grasp your belt, if you're wearing one. If the road surface is grated, face it, place your hands in the grate, and hold on. Drawbridges typically take several minutes to open completely, giving you time to brace yourself.

5 Wait.

Depending on the height of the vessel moving under the bridge, the span may not move to a completely vertical position. Even in its fully open condition, however, the span will not move beyond 90 degrees, so you will not be hanging upside down. Wait until the ship passes and the bridge span lowers, then walk off the bridge. Your car will have slid down the open span and crashed into the joint where it meets the horizontal section of the roadway.

6 If you begin to lose your grip or cannot find a hand-hold, jump.

Though any high fall into water should be considered only as a last resort, you stand a better chance of avoiding major injury when landing in water than landing on the road surface. Because the bridge is over a shipping channel, the water below you should be deep enough for you to avoid hitting the bottom. Look down to make sure the ship is not directly below the bridge, then jump as soon as you can, before the opening span adds elevation to your leap and before the ship is so close that you cannot get out of its way. Keep your legs and feet together, point your toes, and place your arms straight above your head.

7 After breaking the surface, open your arms and legs wide to slow your descent.

8 Head for shore.
Immediately swim up and away from the path of the approaching ship as fast as you can.

Face the grated roadway and hold on.

HOW TO LAND A HELICOPTER IF THE ENGINE FAILS

When a helicopter's engine stalls, it cannot be restarted in mid-flight. The helicopter's low flying altitude (usually 500 to 1,000 feet) means you will have just seconds to react before it crashes to earth. A controlled emergency landing after engine failure, called autorotation, uses the weight of the helicopter and its downward trajectory to move air across the blades. The air causes the main rotor to rotate enough to give you some lift and slow your descent to a controlled rate. At an elevation of 500 feet, you will hit the ground in about 20 seconds. You will not have time to use the radio to call for help. Perform the following steps carefully but immediately.

1 Locate the critical flight controls.
- COLLECTIVE. This is a lever to the pilot's left that controls the helicopter's altitude. Moving the collective slightly changes the pitch angle of the blades, which in turn changes the helicopter's angle of attack, allowing it to climb or descend.
- PEDALS. The two pedals (left and right) control the pitch of the tail rotor, which prevents the helicopter body from spinning in the opposite direction from the main rotor. The pedals are used to move the helicopter left and right during flight.

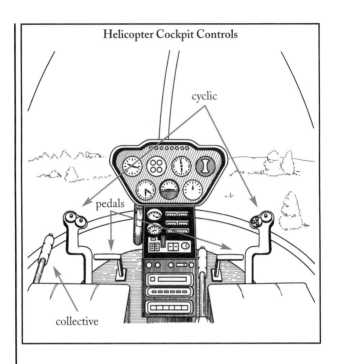

Helicopter Cockpit Controls

cyclic

pedals

collective

- **Cyclic.** This stick, directly in front of the pilot, controls the tilt of the rotor disk, which allows the helicopter to move forward or backward.

2 Lower the collective.

Move the collective lever all the way down to its lowest position. This will cause the helicopter to descend (if it isn't already), but it will allow the air moving over the blades to turn the rotor. You will have only about one second to fully lower the collective after engine cutout before the helicopter becomes completely uncontrollable.

3 Place your feet on the pedals.

The left pedal will move the helicopter to the left, the right will move it right. Though you will have minimal forward motion, you should be able to use the pedals to move the helicopter in either direction to position it for a safer landing. The pedals are extremely sensitive, so do not put too much pressure on them.

4 Glide.

While an airplane will glide forward about 20 feet for every 1 foot it descends (a glide ratio of 20:1), a helicopter's glide ratio is just 4:1, so you will not be able to move forward very far before hitting the ground. Look for a smooth surface and keep a slow forward speed. Ideally, you should set the helicopter down in an empty parking lot or other paved, open space free of people, cars, power lines, and other obstructions. Avoid landing in a field: The landing skids may catch on rocks, stumps, or mud, causing the helicopter to slide or flip over. Do not attempt a water landing. Make sure you are strapped in to the seat.

5 Pull the collective all the way up.

At about 50 feet above the ground, keep the helicopter level and pull the collective all the way up to cushion the ground contact as much as possible.

6 Prepare for impact.

When properly executed, an autorotation will bring the helicopter to the ground at about 20 mph, slow enough for the impact to be easily survivable. However, the blades on the main rotor will bend downward from the impact, and may slice through the tail boom and/or hit the ground and snap off. Get on the floor of the cabin as soon as you feel impact, then run from the cabin, which may explode, as soon as there is no danger of being hit by the rotor blades.

Be Aware

Performing an autorotation above and then landing in tall trees (which offer a relatively flexible and cushioned landing surface) may protect occupants, but will probably destroy the helicopter.

CHAPTER 5
SURVIVING THE ELEMENTS

HOW TO SURVIVE IF YOU ARE STRANDED ON AN ICEBERG

1 Construct a shelter.

For protection from the harsh climate, you must build a snow shelter immediately. Your iceberg should have plentiful amounts of snow, so construct either a snow cave (make a huge pile of snow, hollow it out, and crawl inside) or a snow trench (dig a deep channel in the snow, cover the top by stacking snow blocks or improvising a tarp out of materials on hand, and crawl in). A snow trench requires less energy and time to construct, but will limit your range of movement and should be used only if you expect quick rescue.

2 Melt snow and ice to make water.

Place snow in a container and melt over a flame to create drinkable water. If snow is not available, scrape shavings from the topmost layer of ice. Though sea ice contains salt, over time the salt leeches from the ice due to surface melt, and the water from the top ice should be safe for drinking.

3 Cross icebergs to get closer to land.

Wind and ocean currents will keep icebergs in motion, often causing them to crash into one another. Step onto a new iceberg if it will bring you closer to a land mass. Use caution when crossing; the edges may be very slick, and the ice may be thin and prone to cracking or collapse. Do not jump onto a new iceberg. Test the strength of the ice by pressing lightly with a foot, then adding pressure slowly until you are certain it can support your weight.

4 Catch fish and seabirds.
Fashion a fishing rod with anything available (harpoon, spear, ski pole, or walking stick) and use it for fishing. Seabirds congregate on icebergs, and may be killed with ice balls.

Do not try to reach across icebergs.

5 Look for seals.
Seals eat fish, and you may be able to scare one away from a fresh catch. As a last resort, if you're not likely to be rescued for a while and can't cross to another iceberg, and only if your life is at risk, consider killing a seal. Seals can serve both as food and as a source of fuel. Unless there is surface melt, without a fuel source you will be unable to melt snow and ice for drinking water and you will quickly die of dehydration. (Avoid sucking on ice: It will lead to hypothermia.) Seals will occasionally jump on drifting icebergs to escape predators and may pop up through breath holes in the ice. While out of the water, seals are generally inactive and docile. Approach adults stealthily from the rear and kill using a club, harpoon, or homemade spear to the skull.

6 Make fuel from seal blubber.
Cut blubber (fat) from the seal carcass and place in the best bowl you can fashion. Using an implement, pound the blubber until it liquifies. Roll a small piece of material into a wick, place it in the blubber, and light.

7 Roast or boil seal meat for food.

8 Burn moist seal skins to create smoky signal fires during the day.
However, your best chance of polar rescue is from land. Just because a ship can see you on an iceberg does not mean it can rescue you.

Be Aware

- Small penguins are also a good food source. Penguins have most of their strength in their flippers, however, so avoid being bashed by a flipper when hunting by approaching from the rear and pinning wings to the sides. Avoid attacking from the front or you risk being badly "beaked."

- In Antarctica, which is a frozen landmass surrounded by ice, icebergs tend to drift in a clockwise pattern around the South Pole, pushed by the circumpolar current. An iceberg may eventually pass a populated weather station or move into a shipping channel. (Weather and research stations may be located hundreds of miles apart in polar regions.) In the Arctic, which is a frozen sea, the currents also move clockwise, east to west, around the polar ice cap. However, the transpolar drift, a current that carries water and ice eastward from Siberia, may bring an iceberg down the east coast of Greenland into more populated areas. The trip from the edge of the Arctic to Greenland may take several months.

HOW TO SURVIVE
A FLASH FLOOD

In a Car

⭐ Watch cars in front of you.
If you see drivers stalling, or notice water reaching halfway up car wheels, do not proceed.

⭐ Estimate the water depth.
Water may be deeper than it appears. A car will stall (and float) in six inches of water. If you are unsure if a road is safe to drive through, get out of your car and check the water level using a stick.

⭐ Exit the vehicle immediately if the car stalls or begins to float.
If the door will not open, crawl out the window (you may need to break a power window if the car's electronics become saturated).

⭐ Walk or run to safety.
Get to higher ground as fast as possible.

⭐ Float.
If you are knocked off your feet by the rushing water, cover your head with your arms and attempt to float on your back, feet first, until you can grab a stationary object and climb to safety.

Exit the vehicle immediately if the car stalls or begins to float.

At Home

⭐ Call for help.
When you see floodwaters heading toward your house, seek help. Because of the risk of electric shock, avoid using a wired telephone if there is water in the house. Use a cellular phone.

⭐ Observe the water level.
If the water outside is less than six inches deep, and you are able to walk without falling down, move to higher ground. If walking is impossible, go back inside.

⭐ Move to the highest floor.
If the house is three or more stories, move to a high floor. If the house is two stories or less, get on the roof.

⭐ Signal rescuers.
Use a whistle, wave a white T-shirt or another piece of clothing, or shout to make your presence known. Continue to call for help until you are rescued or the waters recede.

Be Aware
• If time permits, quickly gather these supplies and place them in a plastic bag: flashlight with spare batteries; battery-operated radio; first-aid kit; rope; whistle; gallon of water; bread, granola bars, or other nonperishable, high-carbohydrate

foodstuffs; essential medications. Take them with you when you leave your house.

- Do not eat or drink any foods that have been touched by floodwaters. The packaging may harbor dangerous germs or chemicals.
- When reentering a flooded building, wear boots and waders, and watch for snakes.
- Pump out flooded basements gradually (approximately one-third of the water per day) to avoid sudden structural damage.
- Have the property checked by a qualified structural engineer before moving back in.

ON FOOT

 Find a flotation device.
Put on a life jacket, inflate a pool toy, or grab a foam (not down or cotton) sofa cushion. Wood floats, but a large piece of furniture may be unwieldy and difficult to carry.

 Run.
Get to high ground or a high floor of a multistory building immediately. Avoid low-lying areas such as spillways, areas near storm drains, and creeks and riverbanks. Before crossing flooded open areas and streets, watch for floating objects (trees, cars, appliances) that might knock you down.

⭐ Check shallow water.

If the water is less than six inches deep and not moving quickly, you should be able to walk quickly or run. The water level may rise quickly, however, and fast-moving water can knock you down. Prepare to move fast.

⭐ Move to the roof.

If you are trapped by rising, fast-moving water and cannot get to higher ground, get on the roof of a two- or three-story house. Avoid the first and second floors, as these may become inundated quickly.

Be Aware

Do not attempt to swim across floodwaters. Deep, quickly moving floodwaters will almost certainly overpower you and sweep you away. You will be unable to see large objects, such as trees, that may be carried by the water, and you may be struck by them.

HOW TO SURVIVE
A MUD SLIDE

1 Run perpendicular to the slide.
You cannot outrace a mud slide. Run across the terrain and seek high ground.

2 Avoid riverbeds.
Mud and debris flows generally travel in the channels made by rivers, creeks, and streams (though the slide may be wider than the channel), so move away from these areas as quickly as possible.

3 Seek shelter.
If you do not have time to escape the slide, get inside a building—preferably one made of concrete, stone, or brick—that has a foundation. Avoid mobile homes, cabins on concrete pilings, and other structures that are not built into the ground, as they cannot withstand the force of the debris flow and will likely be severely damaged or carried away.

4 Move to an upper floor.
Mud and debris may penetrate windows and walls of lower floors. Get to a second or third story for added protection.

Run perpendicular to the slide.

5 Take cover.

Get under a desk, large table, or other heavy piece of furniture to protect you from falling objects should the slide rock the structure or knock it from its foundation.

How to Detect an Imminent Mud Slide

1 Monitor creeks and streams.

Fast-rising water levels in mountain waterways indicate there have been large amounts of rainfall that can cause mud slides or debris flows. If you notice that streams and creeks are overflowing their banks or have become brown and muddy, expect a slide. Deforested areas and those recently burned are prone to mud slides. Note any barren or blackened land at a higher elevation than your position.

2 Listen.

Mud slides begin with rainwater but quickly pick up dirt, rocks, trees, and other objects, giving the debris flow an unmistakable rumbling sound as it quickly moves downhill. A loud, sustained rumble indicates that a mud slide is approaching.

HOW TO LEAVE A TRAIL FOR RESCUERS IF YOU ARE LOST IN THE WILDERNESS

1 Walk through "track traps."

Mud pools, wet sandy areas, snow, and other soft terrain can hold footprints for long periods (days or weeks, between storms). Step in these areas, write "HELP," and draw arrows to signal your direction of travel to potential rescuers. If you reverse course, step in the tracks again on your way out. Your footprints will indicate that the search should not continue past the track trap.

2 Build campfires.

Smoke from campfires can be seen for miles, and fires show up well at night. Warm fire rings also indicate to rescuers that you were recently in a particular area. Do not leave fires burning, but make sure coals or dirt are still warm when you leave. (Warm coals can reignite, so leave warm fire rings only in wet areas or under conditions of low fire danger.)

3 Follow roads and rivers.

Rescuers will use natural boundaries to limit their search area. Do not cross roads or rivers. Rather, follow them to more populated areas. Do not climb steep slopes unless you must: Your searchers will follow, delaying your rescue.

Step in soft terrain to signal rescuers.

Form an arrow to mark your direction.

how to leave a trail for rescuers if you are lost in the wilderness

4 **Leave markers.**

If you abandon marked trails, signal your direction of travel by turning over fresh vegetation or leaving small piles of rocks.

5 **Listen carefully.**

In addition to shouting your name, searchers may use a "call word," an unusual word yelled back and forth to distinguish members of the search party from the victim when not in the line of sight. Listen for odd words ("Hoboken," "spaghetti," "Internet") that sound out of place in the wilderness.

6 **Yell loudly and make noises in groups of three.**

Three calls is the international distress signal. Use a whistle, if available, to signal your position.

7 **Sleep lightly.**

A rescue party may continue during the night, so use a flashlight or head lamp. Look for flashlights and listen for searchers between naps.

8 **Leave personal items behind.**

If you are lost in warm weather and have excess clothing or supplies, leave small items along your path as a signal to rescuers. Traveling light will also make hiking easier.

9 **Use a mirror to signal to air searchers.**

A mirror or other reflective device will help rescuers in planes or helicopters locate your position. Special "survival" mirrors with a hole in the center are especially effective in focusing sunlight.

CHAPTER 6

EVERYDAY DANGERS

HOW TO ESCAPE
A WILD TAXI RIDE

⭐ Claim you have no money.
Tell the cabbie you forgot your wallet. The ride should end immediately.

⭐ Light a cigarette.
Tell the cabbie that his driving is making you nervous and light a cigarette (or a cigar, for better results). Smoking in cabs is usually illegal and your driver may stop the car.

⭐ Threaten to vomit.
Inform the cabbie that his driving is making you sick. There are few things cabbies like less than a passenger who vomits in the backseat. The driver may ask you to exit the cab.

⭐ Use your cell phone.
Make a loud show of pretending to call police (or the local taxi commission) and reporting the driver's name and license/medallion number. The driver will want to get rid of you as soon as possible.

⭐ Run.
If the cab stops at a light, open the door and take off.

Protect your head with your bag or briefcase.

 Jump.

If the driver will not stop, wait until the cab approaches a turn or slows for a light. As the driver brakes, open the door on the side of the cab facing the sidewalk. Do not bail out into traffic. Tuck your chin to your chest, cover your head with your hands, and jump out of the car. Roll away from the taxi in a somersault position, protecting your head with your arms. If you have a bag or leather briefcase, hold it on top of your head for added protection. Make sure your path takes you away from the rear wheels. The cab's forward momentum will cause you to roll for several yards before coming to a stop.

HOW TO SURVIVE A FALL DOWN A STREET GRATING

1 Bend your knees.

The moment you feel the grating beneath you begin to give way, bend your knees. Your legs will act as shock absorbers, flexing on impact.

2 Hold your arms close to your body.

Do not fling your arms out and attempt to grab anything on your way down. Your hands or wrists may catch on something and break as you descend.

3 Prepare for impact.

Unless the grating is over a sewer line or subway tunnel, you will probably only fall about 10 feet. Most gratings on the sidewalk are used to allow sunlight to enter one floor below grade.

4 Land.

Land in a crouch on the balls of your feet, not flat-footed, on your heels, nor on your rear end. Bend your knees further, absorbing impact with your quads (thigh muscles). Do not use your hands to break your fall.

5 Roll onto your shoulder.

After impact, avoid pitching forward by immediately rolling onto your shoulder, provided there is room to do so.

6 Look for a ladder.

Some gratings have ladders, especially those over subways, sewers, or utility tunnels. Find one and climb out.

HOW TO SURVIVE
WHEN TRAPPED
IN A SEWER

1 Find a light source.

Sewers are usually pitch-black over long stretches and navigation will be impossible without some type of light. Use a flashlight, penlight, LED from a cell phone or car key, matches, or a lighter to see. Although sewer gases are generally not combustible in the concentrations found in mains, use an open flame light source as a last resort. If you have no light source, look upward for daylight reaching the sewer main through storm drain inlets, gratings in the street, or the small holes in (or around the rims of) manhole covers. Head to the light source: Generally it will lead to a way out or a place where you can communicate with the surface.

2 Stand straight and tall.

Bacteria breaking down organic material create hydrogen sulfide (H_2S), which is responsible for the "rotten egg" odor in sewers. While the foul smell is distasteful, in small concentrations the gas is not deadly (though high concentrations can be fatal). In addition, hydrogen sulfide is slightly heavier than air and will tend to be in higher concentrations lower in the sewer pipe. Keep your head as high as possible, near the top (or "crown") of the pipe. Covering your nose and mouth with a handkerchief may provide minimal relief.

3 Wait until late at night to move.
Large, combined sewer systems—those that aggregate household wastewater and storm water—generally have their highest flows after breakfast and after dinner, when toilets are flushed and dishes are washed, and during or just after rainstorms. Flows will be lowest, and navigation and movement easiest, in the middle of the night. Wait until 2 or 3 A.M. to begin your escape, unless it is raining and the system is filling with storm runoff. Expect a sewage depth of 12 to 18 inches in the middle of the night, and up to 36 inches during busier periods. The deeper the flow, the greater the forces acting on you will be, making it harder for you to maintain balance.

4 Check the direction of the flow.
Sewers move wastewater downhill, using gravity. Smaller diameter pipes enter the system upstream and connect to larger and larger mains as you move downstream in the system. Locate a larger main (72 or 92 inches in diameter) and establish the directional flow of the sewage.

5 Move upstream.
Though it seems counterintuitive, move upstream toward smaller pipes. Larger mains downstream will contain older sewage, which has been broken down by bacteria over a longer period of time. These

downstream pipes will have much higher levels of hydrogen sulfide, which may be deadly. Instead, move upstream to areas with fresher sewage and lower concentrations of gas.

6 | Watch your step.
The floor and walls of the sewer will be coated with slime and will be extremely slippery. There may also be a channel in the center of the pipe to accelerate the flow of sanitary sewage. Walking in this channel will be difficult, so keep to the sides of the main.

7 | Observe the behavior of rats and cockroaches.
Though both rats and cockroaches can swim, they prefer dry land and are likely to be on ledges above the sewage flow, on walls (for roaches), and in your path. As you walk, check the concentration of rats and especially roaches: Both serve as your early warning system of danger in the sewer. The presence of rats in large numbers can be a good sign. Rats indicate that the air is safe to breathe, even near the bottom of the sewer main. If you notice a sharp increase in the number of rats and roaches, or see them heading past you upstream, dangerous conditions exist downstream—a broken pipe or a full siphon may be causing sewage to back up toward your position. If they begin scurrying past you, be ready to move upstream quickly, away from the problem.

Rats will indicate that the air is safe to breathe.

8 Locate a lateral storm sewer.

Look for a relatively dry main entering the combined main; this is a storm sewer "lateral" and should be easier to walk in, with lower levels of gas and odor. The lateral pipe may be smaller in diameter (48 inches, perhaps less), so be prepared to kneel or crawl. Look up for an overhead storm sewer grate or inlet. Push it up and to the side, then slide it over and climb out or yell for help. If you cannot find a lateral main, or cannot access the inlet, continue to step 9.

9 Locate a manhole cover.

Listen for traffic and street noise above you. If you see light entering the sewer main from above and hear the pounding of cars, you will likely be under a manhole cover. Look for iron rungs built into the wall leading up 10 to 20 feet to the manhole cover. Use caution when climbing: Another byproduct of sewage decomposition is sulfuric acid, which over time may have disintegrated the cast-iron rungs leading to the manhole.

10 Open the manhole cover.

The cover may weigh 150 pounds or more. Wait until the traffic noise subsides, push the manhole cover up slightly at one edge, then slide it over. Watch for traffic as you climb out. If you cannot locate or lift a manhole cover, continue to step 11.

11 Bang on pipes.

In the main or lateral sewer, look for smaller diameter (12 inches or less) metal pipes emptying into larger mains. These "household" sewer connections enter the sewer from homes and buildings. Bang on one to signal someone on the surface and/or in the connected building. Metal pipe carries sound very efficiently.

12 Plug a pipe.

If you cannot escape and banging does not bring rescuers, use your shirt, a piece of wood, or another object to block a household pipe where it enters the sewer. The sewage will begin backing up into the building, and eventually someone will access the sewer to investigate the blockage.

Be Aware

- Water and sewer department personnel are more likely to be working on smaller pipes further up the system than larger (72- or 92-inch) mains near the downstream end. Your best chance of finding people is in the smaller pipes.
- In high concentrations, hydrogen sulfide deadens your olfactory senses. If you smell hydrogen sulfide (rotten egg smell) and then suddenly stop smelling it—particularly if you are moving downstream— the concentration of the gas may have increased dramatically. Speed up your efforts to escape.
- Do not drink any liquids found in the sewer, even if the sewer carries only rainwater runoff. If sewage inadvertently enters your body through an orifice, or via cuts or skin abrasions (no matter how minor), seek medical treatment as soon as you escape.

HOW TO FALL DOWN A FLIGHT OF STAIRS

1 Lower your center of gravity.
When you sense yourself falling, crouch low to the floor.

2 Do not attempt to break your fall.
Avoid using your hands to try to break your initial fall. The weight of your body, in conjunction with the gravitational forces of the fall, may break your wrists.

3 Move to the inside wall.
As you fall, keep your body close to the wall of the stairway, if there is one. You are more likely to catch an arm or a leg in the banister (or fall through or over it) than to injure yourself on the wall.

4 Tuck.
Move your arms, legs, hands, and knees in close to your body. Tuck your chin to your chest. With your elbows tucked in, place your hands on the sides of your head.

5 Roll in a zigzag pattern.
Concentrate on rolling on your major muscle groups: lats (back), deltoids (shoulders), quads (thighs), and gluteus maximus (rear end). Avoid rolling head

Roll in toward the wall on one shoulder,
then out toward the banister on the other.

over heels, straight down: Your increasing momentum
may cause injury, even with your body positioned correctly. Instead, roll in toward the wall on one shoulder, then out toward the banister on the other. Repeat
the pattern until you reach the bottom. A zigzag roll
will help you reduce speed and maintain control. Do
not attempt the zigzag roll on a stairway with an old,
rickety banister, an open railing, or no banister at all.

6 Check for injury.
Do not get up immediately. Slowly move each limb in
turn to make sure nothing is broken. If you are in
extreme pain, yell for help.

HOW TO SURVIVE
A FLU PANDEMIC

★ Wear a surgical mask in public.
Influenza is a virus that enters the body through contact with mucous membranes, so you must protect your nose and mouth. If you cannot get a mask, keep a bandanna tied securely over your nose and mouth. Do not touch or rub your eyes, nose, or mouth.

★ Restrict and ration towel usage.
Each member of the household should have an assigned towel, washcloth, dishcloth, and pillow. (All household members should sleep in separate bedrooms, if possible.) Label towels with masking tape to avoid mix-ups. Wash all towels with bleach.

★ Sneeze and cough into your elbow.
Sneezing and coughing into your elbow will prevent germs from reaching your hands and being spread through contact. Recommend that others follow suit.

★ Keep your hands clean.
When washing hands in a public restroom, first pull the lever on the towel dispenser to lower a towel, then wash your hands. Rip off the dispensed towel, then use it to pull the dispenser lever again and to turn off the water faucet. Discard the first towel. Tear off the second towel and use it to dry your hands and open the bathroom door, then discard.

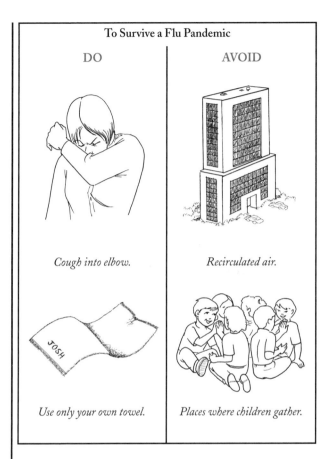

To Survive a Flu Pandemic

DO	AVOID
Cough into elbow.	*Recirculated air.*
Use only your own towel.	*Places where children gather.*

 Sanitize before touching areas with high germ potential.

Disinfect light switches, doorknobs, keyboards and mice, telephone receivers, refrigerator door handles, sink faucets, and the flush handle on the toilet. Do not use public telephones.

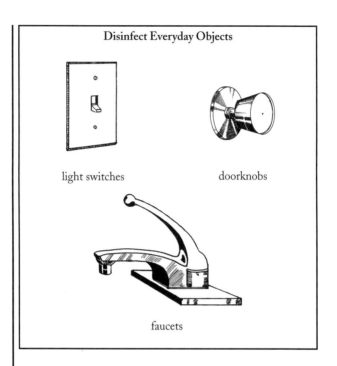

Disinfect Everyday Objects

light switches

doorknobs

faucets

⭐ Empty the trash often.
Do not let used tissues pile up in wastebaskets; they may carry the flu. Wear rubber gloves when emptying trash. Wash the gloves frequently, or throw them out after each use and get a new pair.

⭐ Avoid areas with recirculated air systems.
Do not get on an airplane. Avoid entering buildings that use recirculation systems designed to reduce fuel consumption. (In the United States, many such structures were erected during the 1970s energy crisis.)

✪ **Do not enter areas where people congregate.**
Hospitals, prisons, day-care centers, college dorms, movie theaters, checkout lines, and other places where large numbers of people cohabitate or group closely together should be avoided during the pandemic.

Be Aware
- Get a flu shot as soon as they become available.
- Wash hands frequently and immediately upon returning home from being outdoors.
- Not all masks are equally effective. For best protection, use an N95 "respirator" mask that completely covers the nose, mouth, and chin.

HOW TO STITCH A GAPING WOUND

You will need 3 clean, dry hand towels or other cloths, clean water, tweezers, small pliers, scissors, a high-proof liquor (preferably vodka or gin), diphenhydramine (a liquid antihistimine), a sewing needle, unused fishing line or dental floss, and tissues.

1 **Stop the bleeding.**
Hold one of the hand towels over the wound for 15 minutes, using firm pressure. Do not use a tourniquet because you will cut off the blood supply and may force an amputation. Raise the affected limb above the level of the heart to slow bleeding. Do not attempt to stitch the wound until bleeding is under control.

2 **Clean the wound.**
Soak the injured body part in warm water. Gently scrub the wound, taking care not to dislodge any obvious blood clots. Irrigate by running cool water over the wound for 5 minutes.

3 **Inspect the wound carefully for foreign material.**
Use tweezers to remove any foreign objects, then irrigate again. (Remember the phrase: "The solution to pollution is dilution.")

*Grip the needle with the pliers so that
the needle's point curves upward.*

*Enter the skin ¹/₄ inch from the wound's edge.
Pull the needle through the skin using the pliers.*

*Wrap two loops of thread from the "needle" side of the thread
around the nose of your pliers. Grab the 2-inch tail
of the thread with your pliers and gently pull it through
the looped thread to create the knot.*

4 Sterilize your equipment.
Wash the needle, tweezers, pliers, and scissors in hot, soapy water. Rinse once with warm water, then again with alcohol. Lay the tools to dry on one of the towels.

5 Wash your hands.
Lather for at least 5 minutes.

6 Prepare the victim.
Instruct the victim to lie down on a table or the floor, preferably on his back. Do not allow the victim to sit or stand. Rinse the wound again with warm water and pat it dry. Splash lightly with alcohol and wait 3 minutes. Pour several capfuls of the diphenhydramine directly into the wound to provide some anesthesia.

7 Prepare a clean work space.
Cut a hole in the center of the third towel. Place this "smock" over the wound, making sure the complete wound is visible through the hole.

8 Prepare the needle and thread.
Using the pliers, bend the needle into a "C" shape. Measure out ten times the length of the wound in fishing line or dental floss. Cut. Run the "thread" through the eye of the needle so the needle rests one-quarter of the way down the thread. Rewash your hands.

9 | Make the first stitch.

You should "throw" the first stitch at the midpoint of the wound. First, grip the needle with the pliers, clamping over the needle's hole. Next, hold the pliers so that the needle's point curves upward. Turn your wrist and aim the point directly down at the skin. Use your other hand to hold up the wound edge with the tweezers. Finally, enter the skin $1/4$ inch from the wound's edge, come through the wound, enter the other side of the wound's edge, and come out $1/4$ inch from the other edge of the wound.

10 | Knot each stitch.

Pull the needle through the skin using the pliers, then pull the thread with your hand until 2 inches are left on the side where the needle entered the skin. Loosely wrap two loops of thread from the "needle side" of the thread around the nose of your pliers. Grab the 2-inch tail with your pliers, then apply gentle upward pressure to bring both edges of the wound together. Pull your pliers back through the looped floss to create the knot, pulling gently in opposite directions so the knot lies flat on the skin.

11 | Lock the knot.

Quickly arc your pliers-hand toward the needle side of the thread and pull both ends of the thread down onto the skin. Doing so "locks" the knot and moves the knot onto the skin rather than over the wound.

12 | Secure the knot.
Repeat the looping and knotting five times, alternating the direction of the looping; this will avoid "granny" knots that will not hold. If you notice that your hands are alternating back and forth in a rhythmic pattern as you tie each knot, you are tying correctly. Double-check that the knot is pulled to the side so that it lays over the skin, not on the wound itself.

13 | Cut the thread.
Cut both ends of thread. Leave a $1/4$-inch tail of thread so the stitching can be removed later.

14 | Continue stitching.
Choose the midpoint between the first stitch and one end of the wound and repeat steps 10 through 14. Continue to bisect the wound between stitches, throwing additional stitches and tying knots until the wound is closed.

HOW TO FREE YOUR LEG FROM A BEAR TRAP

1 Move your foot and wiggle your toes.

Bear traps are designed to catch and hold the leg of a bear, not cut it off. Your leg may be badly bruised, but it should not be severely injured or amputated. Attempt to move your foot and toes to determine if you still have circulation and to check for tendon and muscle damage. In general, the steel "jaws" of the trap are not sharp. Each side of the jaw should have "teeth" that are designed to allow circulation. If you cannot feel your foot or do not have range of movement, you will have to work quickly.

2 Sit with the trap in front of you.

Sit on the ground and move the trapped leg so it is in front of you, bent slightly. The trap may be anchored to the ground with a short chain, or the chain may be attached to a loose hook. (When the caught animal runs away, the hook leaves a trail that is easy to track.)

3 Familiarize yourself with the trap.

The trap will have one piece of bent steel (a "spring") to the left and another piece to the right of the jaws. The center of the trap will have a flat steel plate called a "pan." Your leg will be between the jaws, your foot on the pan.

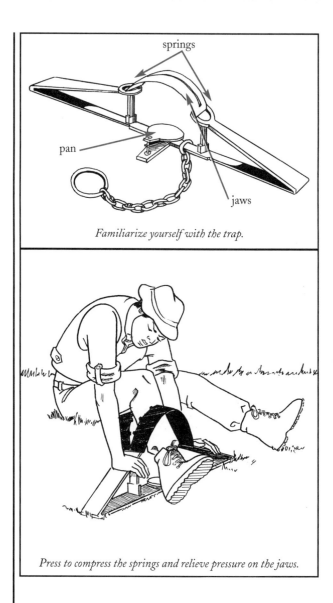

Familiarize yourself with the trap.

Press to compress the springs and relieve pressure on the jaws.

4 Place one hand on the top of each spring.

5 Close the springs.
With as much force as possible, press down hard on the springs to compress them. As the springs compress, they will lower and relieve pressure on the jaws.

6 Once the jaws are loose, slip your foot out of the trap.

7 Release the springs.
Take pressure off the springs slowly to avoid snapping the jaws closed suddenly.

8 Check your leg for damage.
Look for broken skin and tissue damage. Seek medical attention if you are injured. Be sure to request a tetanus booster if metal has pierced the skin.

HOW TO SAVE YOURSELF IF YOU ARE HAVING A HEART ATTACK

1 Chew aspirin.

As soon as you suspect a heart attack, thoroughly chew and swallow one 325-mg aspirin tablet, or four 81-mg baby aspirins. For best effect, do not swallow the aspirin whole. Heart attacks occur when the blood vessels supplying oxygen to the heart muscle become clogged. Aspirin will not stop the heart attack or remove the blockage, but it will prevent blood clotting cells (platelets) from adding to the blockage.

2 Alert others.

If possible, tell people around you that you are having a heart attack. Instruct them to call emergency services.

3 Decrease the heart's oxygen consumption.

Stop all activity. The faster your heart pumps, the more oxygen it uses up. Think calming thoughts about bringing your heart rate down to one beat per second. If you have a watch with a second hand, focus on the second hand. For each second think or say quietly "heart-beat." Repeat.

4 | Increase oxygen delivery to the heart.
Lie down on the ground. Elevate your legs to keep as much blood pooled around your heart as possible; this will decrease the work your heart must do to pump blood. Open the windows to increase the room's oxygen level. If you have access to an oxygen tank, place the nasal cannula under your nose, turn the knob to 4 liters (or until you feel air coming through the nasal prongs), and take deep, slow breaths through your nose and out your mouth.

5 | Perform cough-CPR.
Breathe, then cough every three seconds. Take a breath in through your nose, think "heart-beat, heart-beat, heart-beat," then cough. Repeat. Coughing will deter fainting and help you stay conscious until conventional CPR can be administered.

Be Aware
Do not consume food or water. You may need a hospital procedure to "unclog" your arteries, and food or liquids in your system complicate treatment.

HOW TO SAVE YOURSELF FROM CHOKING

1 Try to talk.

If you can talk or are able to vocalize in any way, or if you make a sound when coughing, your airway is not completely blocked and you are not in imminent danger of death. Keep coughing to dislodge the stuck material. If you cannot make any sounds, you will need to perform the one-person Heimlich maneuver.

Drop onto a blunt object six inches above your navel to force air up your windpipe.

2 Quickly locate a blunt object at waist level.
If you are indoors, find a chair, table, counter, or other piece of furniture; if you are outside, look for a tall tree stump, fence, ledge, or large rock.

3 Face the object.

4 Bend over the object.
Lean so that the object touches your body six inches above your navel.

5 Fall.
Let yourself drop forward hard and fast onto the object. This movement should force the air up your windpipe and eject the item that is blocking your airway.

Appendix

LAST-DITCH LIQUIDS YOU CAN DRINK

AFTER DISTILLING

- Urine (long-term ingestion can cause problems)
- Blood (human blood may contain hepatitis or HIV, so animal blood is somewhat safer)
- Seawater

AFTER DISINFECTING

- Freshwater creeks/streams
- Toilet tank water (not toilet bowl water), as long as the tank does not have any type of disinfectant, and provided the rubber seal between the tank and bowl is intact and does not leak
- Water from an unknown source

NEVER DRINK

- Ink
- The water in a vinyl water bed
- Swimming pool water (but OK for bathing)
- Water in a hot tub (but OK for bathing)

LAST-DITCH FOODS
YOU CAN EAT

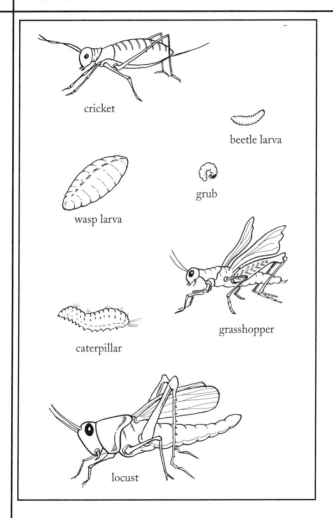

cricket

beetle larva

wasp larva

grub

grasshopper

caterpillar

locust

FIVE CRITICAL KNOTS

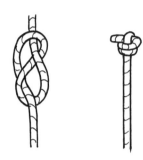

FIGURE 8

Used to keep the end of a rope from running out, as through a pulley on a boat.

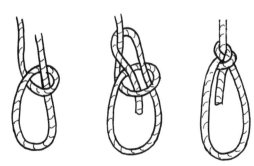

BOWLINE

Used to make a small, nonslipping loop to secure around an object.

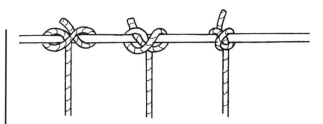

CONSTRICTOR

Used for securing a load. May be difficult to untie when pulled tight.

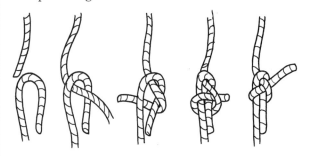

SHEET BEND

Typically used to join two ropes together.

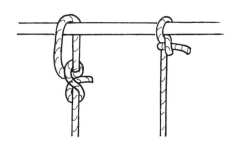

TWO HALF HITCHES

Used in mooring a boat.

THE EXPERTS

Nena Barlow runs Sedona Jeep School (www.sedonajeep school.com), a four-wheel drive instruction and guide service in Sedona, Arizona. She has been driving off-road since 1976.

Charles L. Barr is the author of *Welcome to Texas: Avoiding the Sting of Fire Ants,* a publication of the extension service of Texas A&M University.

Bruce Beach (www.webpal.org) trained as a radiological scientific officer in the 1960s and has built dozens of nuclear survival shelters. He is the coordinator of Ark Two, the world's largest privately owned survival complex.

Carrie Brewer is an actor, stuntwoman, fight choreographer, and stage combat instructor in New York City. She is founder and co–artistic director of the Lady Cavalier Theatre Company (www.ladycavaliers.com).

Brennen Brunner is a cold climate survival expert and super-visor of field safety for the U.S. Antarctic Program. He works with the U.S. Air Force's Barren Land Survival Training Program in Greenland and serves as a mountain guide in Alaska and Washington for Alpine Ascents International.

Peggy Callahan is the founder and executive director of the Wildlife Science Center (www.wildlifesciencecenter.org), a nonprofit training, research, and education center in Forest Lake, Minnesota. She has studied captive gray wolves and participated in wolf radio-collaring programs for 20 years.

Around-the-world cyclist Dennis Coello (www.denniscoello.com) has been bike touring since 1965 and mountain biking since testing fat-tire models in the Utah deserts in 1983. He is the author of 13 books and more than 100 articles on various aspects of bicycling.

Cathy Dean, chair of the UK Rhino Group, is director of Save the Rhino International (www.savetherhino.org), a charity committed to ensuring the survival of the rhinoceros species in the wild.

Pat Denevan owns and runs Mission Soaring Center (www.hang-gliding.com), which provides professional hang gliding training in Milpitas, California.

Bastiaan "Bart" Drees, an internationally recognized expert on fire ants, is a professor and extension entomologist at Texas A&M University and the author of *Medical Problems and Treatment for the Red Imported Fire Ant,* among other publications.

Charlie Duchek is chief pilot for Midwest Helicopter (www.flymidwest.com), a helicopter training, rental, and aerial photography company based in Chesterfield, Missouri. He is a certified flight instructor for both airplanes and helicopters.

Dan Egan, one of the world's premier adventure skiers, has appeared in 12 Warren Miller films and has been nominated for 3 Emmy Awards for his own extreme skiing movies. He is the co-founder of Skiclinics (www.skiclinics.com), which coaches extreme skiers and runs ski clinics throughout the world.

Christopher Elliott (www.elliott.org) is *National Geographic Traveler* magazine's ombudsman and a writer for *US News & World Report,* the *New York Times,* and MSNBC. A frequent contributor to National Public Radio, he has written about wild taxi rides and how to survive them.

Floods and Flash Floods, FEMA Fact Sheet, www.fema.gov/hazards/floods/floodf.shtm.

Steve Fettke (www.fettke.com/bungee) teaches and trains bungee jumpers in California and does bungee stunts for film and television. He organized the U.S. Bungee Jumping Championships in 1995 and has competed in the X Games.

Patrick J. Flynn runs En-Fuse Inc. (www.en-fuse.com), an environmental health and training consulting firm. He is a certified environmental trainer with a decade of experience instructing companies on the safe transport, storage, and emergency response to hazardous materials.

Michael Gianetti, an FAA-licensed commercial hot air balloon pilot and pilot instructor, is a certified hot air balloon inspector, repairman, and dealer for new and used balloon systems. He owns Lifecycle Balloons (www.lifecycleballoons.com) in Boulder, Colorado.

Guidance: Potassium Iodide as a Thyroid Blocking Agent in Radiation Emergencies, U.S. Department of Health and Human Services, Food and Drug Administration, Center for Drug Evaluation and Research, November 2001 Procedural.

Dean Gunnarson (www. alwaysescaping.com) is one of the world's foremost escape artists. The first recipient of the Houdini Award, he has escaped from coffins, shark cages, hungry alligators, and a straitjacket while free-falling from an airplane.

Bill Hughes, a hot air balloon pilot and instructor, has been flying balloons and helicopters for 34 years. A former navy pilot, he also served as director of training for American Eagle Airlines. His balloon business (www.blueskyballoons.com) is based in Beacon, New York.

Alexander Jason (www.alexanderjason.com) is a certified crime scene analyst, an expert in the analysis of shooting incidents, and the creator of several videos on the effects of bullets on the human body.

Cory Kufahl owns and runs D-Aces (www.d-aces.com), an extreme stunt motorcycle group and film production company. He has been stunt riding street bikes for 8 years and has performed extreme stunts across the United States and around the world. His latest DVD is *No Mercy*.

Melisa W. Lai., MD, is emergency medicine attending physician at Mt. Auburn Hospital in Cambridge, Massachusetts, and a fellow in medical toxicology at the Massachusetts/ Rhode Island Poison Control Center.

Darren Law (www.darrenlaw.com) is a professional race car driver who served as chief driving instructor at the Bondurant School of High Performance Driving, where he taught precision driving, skid control, and accident avoidance for many years. He drives a Daytona prototype race car in the Rolex Grand Am series.

Tom Mason (www.lugeyourmind.com), the "Bad Boy of Street Luge," is a professional street luge pilot. A stuntman and actor, he has appeared in numerous films and television commercials and is a past winner of the World Extreme Games.

Loui McCurley, a technical specialist for Alpine Rescue in Colorado, works for a rescue equipment manufacturer, consulting on equipment testing, standards, and the performance of rope rescue and access equipment for firefighters, mountain rescuers, and window cleaners.

Vinny Minchillo, an auto enthusiast, demolition derby driver, and lawn-mower racer for 20 years, has survived numerous rollovers and crashes. He has written for *AutoWeek, Sports Car,* and *Turbo* magazines. When not crashing cars, he is an advertising executive in Texas.

Nick Moriarty is founder and director of Ropes Course Developments (www.rcd.co.uk), one of the world's leading ropes course construction and training companies. Ropes Course Developments has constructed more than 400 facilities in 15 countries and trained more than 3,500 ropes course instructors.

Rick Murphy, gorilla keeper, photographer, and research assistant, has studied captive gorilla gestures, vocalizations, and personality differences for more than two decades. He is currently involved in gorilla conservation activities in Rwanda and the Democratic Republic of Congo.

Meryl Nass, MD (www.anthraxvaccine.org), is a practicing internist with expertise in anthrax and biological terrorism. In 1992, she identified the first modern use of biowarfare, and she has criticized the use of current anthrax and smallpox vaccines due to safety concerns. Many of her recommendations for prevention and mitigation of bioterrorism were adopted by the Centers for Disease Control.

Ian Redmond is a naturalist and conservationist who has worked with gorillas and elephants in the wild for decades. He is chief consultant for UNEP/UNESCO's Great Apes Survival Project and currently works with the Born Free Foundation's Elefriends Campaign (www.bornfree.org.uk/elefriends/).

Francis Rizzo is an attorney who has surfed in Long Beach Island, Costa Rica, and Hawaii. He lives outside Philadelphia.

David Scheel is assistant professor of marine biology at Alaska Pacific University and is the principal investigator on the university's Giant Octopus Research Team (www.marine.alaska pacific.edu/octopus/). He has studied the ecology of the Giant Pacific Octopus for 10 years.

Jon Schladweiler (www.sewerhistory.org) is deputy director for the Pima County Wastewater Management Department in Tucson, Arizona. He has three decades of experience in the planning, design, construction, and management of sanitary sewerage facilities. A sewer historian, he runs an exhibit of historical artifacts, photos, and documents depicting the evolution of sewers from prehistory to the present.

Marc Siegel, MD (www.doctorsiegel.com), is an internist and associate professor of medicine at NYU Medical School and the author of *False Alarm: Profiting from the Fear Epidemic*. He is a frequent contributor to the *Nation, New York Times,* and *Los Angeles Times.*

Keith Sutton writes a bimonthly adventure column for ESPNOutdoors.com. A resident of Alexander, Arkansas, he is the author of *Hunting Arkansas: A Sportsman's Guide to the Natural State* and *Catfishing: Beyond the Basics.*

Vampress (www.vampress.net), an aspiring horror personality, creates and maintains a Web resource dedicated to vampire culture in literature and movies. She stalks her victims in the Toronto area, and only bites if asked nicely.

Jack Viorel has lived and surfed on the Northern California coast for 20 years. He has surfed big waves in Australia, Costa Rica, the Dominican Republic, Fiji, Indonesia, Mexico, Nicaragua, and the North Shore.

Ken Zafren, MD, FACEP, is an emergency physician and medical director of the Alaska Mountain Rescue Group. He is on the faculty at Stanford University and has spent more time than he cares to admit on mountain ledges and searching for lost people.

ABOUT THE AUTHORS

JOSHUA PIVEN has wrestled with a giant octopus, escaped from a car perched on the edge of a drawbridge, and survived a spinout at 200 mph. Well, not really, but he could, if he had to. He is the co-author, with David Borgenicht, of the *Worst-Case Scenario Survival Handbook* series.

DAVID BORGENICHT is a writer and armchair adventurer who has survived encounters with mountain lions, alligators, barracudas, and Al Roker. He is the co-author, with Joshua Piven, of the *Worst-Case Scenario Survival Handbook* series and the publisher of Quirk Books.

BRENDA BROWN is an illustrator and cartoonist whose work has appeared in many books and publications, including the *Worst-Case Scenario Survival Handbook* series, *Esquire*, *Reader's Digest*, *USA Weekend*, *21st Century Science & Technology*, the *Saturday Evening Post*, and the *National Enquirer*. Her website is http://webtoon.com.

Visit www.worstcasescenarios.com for updates, new scenarios, and more! Because you just never know. . . .

ACKNOWLEDGMENTS

Josh Piven is extremely grateful to all the gnarly experts for their radical contributions, as well as to his way cool editors Melissa, Jay, and Steve. As always, he thanks his co-author David "Dude" Borgenicht. All you guys rock!

David is grateful for the help of many people involved in the making of this book. Specifically: Jay Schaefer, Steve Mockus, and Melissa Wagner for their wily editing and creative guidance, Frances J. Soo Ping Chow for her design and hair, Brenda Brown for her uniquely wonderful illustrations, and everyone else at Quirk and Chronicle Books for their creativity, loyalty, and friendship. When I think of the countless lives we'll likely save as a result of this book, it warms the cockles of my cold, cold heart and makes me glad to have known you all.

THE FIRST OF THE WORST

⚠ 3 million copies in print

⚠ Translated into 27 languages

⚠ International best-seller

"An armchair guide for the anxious."
—*USA Today*

"The book to have when the killer bees arrive."
—*The New Yorker*

"Nearly 180 pages of immediate action drills for when everything goes to hell in a handbasket."
—*Soldier of Fortune*

"This is a really nifty book."
—*Forbes*

A BOOK FOR EVERY DISASTER

- ⭐ *The Worst-Case Scenario Survival Handbook*
- ⭐ *The Worst-Case Scenario Survival Handbook: Travel*
- ⭐ *The Worst-Case Scenario Survival Handbook: Dating & Sex*

- ⭐ *The Worst-Case Scenario Survival Handbook: Golf*
- ⭐ *The Worst-Case Scenario Survival Handbook: Holidays*
- ⭐ *The Worst-Case Scenario Survival Handbook: Work*

- ⭐ *The Worst-Case Scenario Survival Handbook: College*
- ⭐ *The Worst-Case Scenario Survival Handbook: Weddings*
- ⭐ *The Worst-Case Scenario Survival Handbook: Parenting*
- ⭐ *The Worst-Case Scenario Book of Survival Questions*